Strategic
Planning

Bobb
BIEHL

Strategic Planning

Developing a Strategic Plan
for Your Business, Church, or Organization

Bobb Biehl

AYLEN
PUBLISHING

Aylen.com
1-800-443-1976

978-0-9708623-0-3

Published by Aylen Publishing
Aylen.com
1-800-443-1976

Scripture citations are from the Holy Bible, New International Version, copyright © 1973, 1978, 1984 by International Bible Society; NASB, the New American Standard Bible, © the Lockman Foundation, 1960, 1962, 1963, 1968, 1971, 1972, 1973, 1975, 1977; used by permission; and The Message, the New Testament in Contemporary English, © 1993 by Eugene H. Peterson, published by NavPress, Colorado Springs, Colorado.

Contents

Acknowledgments

———————————————————————————————➤

Thank You

A heartfelt thank you to Cheryl Biehl, my wife, who has been a loyal supporter during the development of the DOCTOR process since we started Masterplanning Group in 1976. Your wise counsel and support have made this material possible and this book a reality. Thank you, Cheryl!

A special thank you to Ed Trenner—my lifelong friend, consulting colleague, and editor—for his invaluable editorial wisdom and sacrificial middle-of-the-night hours invested in the creation of this book. Thank you, Ed!

A sincere thank you to our associates who have each contributed in many ways to the development of the DOCTOR process:

Consulting Associates:

> Terry Fleck—Carmel, Indiana
>
> Gari Mitchell—Littleton, Colorado
>
> Claude Robold—Middletown, Ohio
>
> Ed Trenner—Orange, California

Thank you to all of the pastors who contributed time-tested samples in the appendix of this book for readers to adapt (see list in Appendix section). Thank you for your leadership in the church of our generation!

A deep debt of gratitude to all of our firm's more than 500 clients. Recently I read a saying by a very wise person who observed, "A teacher learns twice." Each client has helped shape this material—as we have taught it, we have also been students. It is hard to feel we are teaching more than we are learning. Thank you one and all!

Introduction

⟶

If you...

are a senior pastor, an executive director, or a president—or if you are a board member, an executive staff member, or a unpaid team member and have plans to be a senior executive or need to work directly with a senior executive—this book is for you.

If you...

feel like you are drifting in a day-to-day survival mode—looking for a way to move from reactive to proactive—this book is for you.

If you...

are an entrepreneurial-style leader who doesn't have an MBA and doesn't want to get bogged down in a cumbersome bureaucratic planning process—this simple planning book is for you.

If you...

have been looking for a step-by-step, proven, profoundly simple process with lots of easily adaptable samples to save you hundreds of hours of staring at blank sheets of paper—this book is for you.

A forest-eye view of this book may be helpful:

1. A proven, six-step planning process (DOCTOR)
2. Ten proven planning tools
3. Over 60 adaptable samples

The essence of these processes, principles, and samples will work for you in a small, medium, or huge church, nonprofit, or for-profit corporation. They will help strengthen the beginning staff and the board of directors. They will work at your next position and your next, helping you with any team you lead. This simple system of planning will help you win 24 hours a day, seven days a week, 52 weeks a year, for the rest of your life.

The Elephant Story

It was eleven o'clock on Friday night. I was sound asleep when the phone rang. On the other end was my friend Duane Pederson, founder of the *Hollywood Free Paper* and now president of Helping Hands Ministries. "How would you like to go to Tucson tomorrow?"

"Tucson?" I groaned, "What in the world would we do in Tucson?"

"My friend, Bobby Yerkes, has a circus playing in Tucson tomorrow and I would like to go down just to get away, clear the cobwebs, and work the circus with him. We'll move some props, have a good time, and be back by ten o'clock tomorrow night."

Now there probably isn't a man or woman alive who hasn't dreamed about running away with the circus as a child, so it didn't take me long to agree to go. Early the next morning at seven o'clock our jet lifted off the runway at Los Angeles International Airport headed for Arizona.

When we got there, it was a hot, dusty, windy day at the fairgrounds where the circus was playing. We moved props from one of the three rings to the next, helped in any way we could, and generally got dusty, dirty, hungry, and tired.

During one of the breaks, I started chatting with a man who trains animals for Hollywood movies. "How is it that you can stake down a 10-ton elephant with the same size stake that you use for this little fellow?" I asked. (The "little fellow" weighed 300 pounds.)

"It's easy when you know two things: elephants really do have great memories, but they aren't very smart. When they are babies, we stake them down. They try to tug away from the stake maybe 10,000 times before they realize that they can't possibly get away. At that point, their 'elephant memory' takes over and they remember for the rest of their lives that they can't get away from the stake."

Humans are sometimes like elephants. When we are teenagers, some unthinking, insensitive, unwise person says, "He's not very good at planning," or "She's not a leader," or "Their team will never make it," and zap, we drive a mental stake into our minds. Often when we become mature adults, we are still held back by some inaccurate one-sentence "stake" put in our minds when we were young leaders.

I sincerely hope that this material will help you pull some of the "stakes" holding you back in the area of planning. Today you are an adult capable of much more than you realize. You are far more capable than you were even 12 months ago, and next year you will be able to do things you can't imagine doing today.

Let's pull some stakes together!

PART ONE

The Planning Process

CHAPTER 1

A Profoundly Simple Planning Process

Chapter Overview

- What is a Strategic Plan?
- Symptoms of Not Having a Strategic Plan
- Benefits of a Clear Plan
- The Essence of the Strategic Planning Process
- Planning is a Continuous Process
- A Plan Needs to Remain Flexible

What Is a Strategic Plan?

If you were to ask the average person how important a Strategic Plan (annual plan, strategic plan) is, they'd likely answer, "Very important." If you ask them, "What is typically included in a Strategic Plan?" they would just as likely answer, "I don't really know."

> ## Definition:
>
> A *Strategic Plan* is a written statement of a group's assumptions about its direction, organization, and cash.

Most leaders have a plan in mind, but not a plan on paper. If it has not been committed to writing, the rest of the staff typically doesn't know the plan. So they make one set of assumptions about the team's future while the leader makes another set of assumptions. This is when you begin to experience conflict. You want to clarify your most basic assumptions in three areas: direction, organization, and cash. If you, your board, and your staff (paid or unpaid team member) are in agreement about these three areas, you are in great shape.

Symptoms of Not Having a Strategic Plan

If your organization lacks a clearly defined, agreed-upon plan, it will likely experience these symptoms:

- "Drifting" day to day. Lack of clear focus. Fire-fighting mode of operation. A leader who feels like s/he isn't really initiating, just responding.

- Lack of preparation for explosive growth. Outgrowing facilities, staff, and funds. Great transitional stress.

- No leadership training program. Leadership is forced to work beyond its experience level, or leadership is virtually nonexistent.

- A team which is making different assumptions. Progressive frustration, tension, and pressure.

- An unclear dream. In a donation-dependent church or nonprofit organization, giving will drop. Without a clear plan, donors don't feel there is a need for their money.

- No clear context for decision making. Paralyzing indecision, a deep stalemate.

Benefits of a Clear Plan

Organizations that develop a clear Strategic Plan find that it:

- increases team spirit because everyone plays off the same sheet of music;

- defines the philosophical framework needed for organizational growth, problem solving, staff orientation, effective communication, and wise decision making;

- reduces organizational frustration, tension, and pressure by putting assumptions in writing.

The Essence of the Strategic Planning Process

To make our profoundly simple planning process easy to remember for our consulting team and our clients, we use the acrostic DOCTOR:

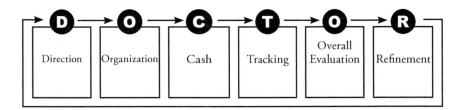

Once you brand the acrostic DOCTOR into your brain along with what each of the words means, you will always know what to do next in the planning process in any sized organization, at any level, anywhere you are in the world, twenty-four hours a day, seven days a week, three hundred sixty-five days a year, for the rest of your life! This is true because the DOCTOR steps are always sequential. You always start with your team's direction first, then you go to organization, then cash, and so on.

Based on this simple DOCTOR acrostic, it is helpful to learn a few profound questions and 10 proven tools to have a solid grasp of the planning process. In chart form the six-step process, combined with the profound questions and key tools for any organization, looks like this:

Process Steps	Profound Questions (fog-cutting questions)	10 Proven Tools
D – Direction	What should we do next? Why?	1. Strategic Planning Arrow
O – Organization	Who is responsible for what? Who is responsible for whom? Do we have the right people in the right places?	2. Organizational chart 3. Position focus sheet
C – Cash	What is our projected income, expense, net? Can we afford it? How can we afford it?	4. Financial health checklist
T – Tracking	Are we on target?	5. Six reporting questions
O – Overall Evaluation	Are we achieving the quality we expect and demand of ourselves?	6. Staff evaluation questionnaire 7. Program evaluation questionnaire 8. Organizational evaluation questionnaire
R – Refinement	How can we be more effective and more efficient (move toward the ideal)?	9. Process charting 10. Annual planning checklist

Planning Is a Continuous Process

Like setting up your first budget, the first year's planning is time consuming, but the next year you review your plan, make a few changes, and you have the new year's plan. It is important, however, to review and update your plan on a regular basis, which leads me to the next point:

A Plan Needs to Remain Flexible

Plans should always remain in "pencil" (or word processing). In your mind see plans as erasable, changeable, or adaptable to tomorrow's realities.

CHAPTER 2

Who Does What in the Planning Process?

Chapter Overview

- Who Is Responsible for What?
- The Strategic Planning Process, Step-by-Step

Note: For most of our illustrations in this book I will use the senior pastor, the church board, and the pastoral staff. Not all readers of this book will identify with or be experienced with business or nonprofit examples. It is my assumption that the principles can be discussed in a church context and the majority of readers will then understand the implications for their church, business, or nonprofit organization.

Who Is Responsible for What?

The area of greatest tension in most organizations is the tension between the board and the senior executive. A high percentage of that tension springs from uncertainty over *who* is responsible for *what*. The sooner you can answer this question for your organization, the better. Here is a very practical way I have found to divide the labor:

The Board

- Frequent names: Board of directors, board of elders, deacons, session, vestry, etc. We will use the term "the board" to represent all of these and you can apply it to fit your situation.

- Primary responsibility: Final decision maker. Final authority. Review, refine, and approve senior executive/staff's draft of the Strategic Plan.

- Result: Organizational stability, wisdom, and balance.

The Senior Executive

- Frequent titles: President, Senior Pastor, Executive Director, or Chief Executive Officer.

- Primary responsibility: Be the staff's directional leader.

- Result: A single vision, unity, and an integrated direction.

A Directional Leader or a Dictator?

A dictator-style leader is a person who leads by saying, "This is what should happen, and this is what's going to happen." He/she is not looking for wise guidance and input, but for a rubber stamp of approval. Her/his first draft of a plan is law.

The directional-style leader says, "I'd like to present to you a draft of the Strategic Plan our team has created. It's the best of our team's thinking, but I'd like you, as a board, to review it, refine it any way you think best, and approve it. Then the staff and I will do our best to carry out the plan and report our progress to you on a regular basis." [Note that while the board has the authority to review, refine, and pass final approval on the Strategic Plan, the senior executive and her/his staff have actually created the draft of the plan. This is more time-efficient than expecting the board to draft the plan in the few hours they are together each year.]

The person selected by the group to be the directional leader—to do draft one of a planning step and present it to the group for their input and approval—typically has the broadest and deepest experience and responsibility within that organization. In a church, these are classic characteristics of a senior pastor.

On a church board you frequently will find people who have far greater non-church experience than the pastor does. One member of the board may own a chain of restaurants. One may have major farms. One member may have set up office buildings all around a three-state area or nationally. But when it comes to actual church experience and understanding of theology, each may say, "I understand business a whole lot better than I understand theology and church work."

A youth pastor may have far greater experience working with youth than the senior pastor does, but the senior pastor is characteristically the person who has the broadest overall experience. S/he has had experience not only with youth, but with Christian education, worship and music, and all of the other aspects of church life. Therefore, in a church it's usually the senior pastor who is asked to draft a Strategic Planning Arrow or an organizational chart.

An exception would be a 23-year-old pastor who may be just coming out of school to serve in a small church. In this setting, a mature board may choose to draft the Strategic Plan. If an organization is temporarily without a senior executive, yet needs a Strategic Plan to know where it is going, someone on the board can draft a Strategic Planning Arrow. But the senior pastor or senior executive is typically the person best qualified to do the first drafts of the planning tools.

THE STAFF

- Frequent names: Executive staff, pastoral staff, administrative team, president's cabinet, etc.

- Primary responsibility: Gives input to Strategic Plan and implements the plan.

- Result: Effectiveness, team spirit, and unity.

The Strategic Planning Process, Step-by-Step

Here's how the Strategic Planning process works:

- ☐ 1. The senior executive completes draft one of each step with input from those involved with, or interested in, each area.

- ☐ 2. The executive staff all agree on the Strategic Plan draft.

- ☐ 3. The senior executive presents draft two to the board for them to review, refine (possibly send back to the drawing boards), and approve.

- ☐ 4. The plan is approved (possibly after several rounds of revisions).

- ☐ 5. The executive staff implements the priorities and reports to the senior executive.

- ☐ 6. The senior executive then reports the staff's progress to the board. In other words, at each board meeting the senior executive comes to the board and says, "Here's the progress we're making on the plan that you approved for us."

Unless your board, your senior executive, and your executive staff are in agreement on who's responsible for what, you are going to have problems. Once you agree on who is responsible for what, it cuts down on frustration, pressure, and tension. When you know that the plan you're working on has been reviewed, refined, and approved by the board, you know that you're not going off in your own direction. When these three levels operate in harmony, it's like playing off the same sheet of music. The whole organization develops at a pace that lets members feel good about working together as a team and not as a bunch of individuals stumbling over each other.

CHAPTER 3

One Time Focus:
Keeping the Big Picture

Fog-Cutting Question:

How do we keep the strategic big picture without getting bogged down in details?

Strategic Planning Arrow*

4 MILESTONES
What major milestones have we already accomplished?

5 IDEAS
What ideas have we had that we should consider turning into goals in the future?

6 ROADBLOCKS
What is keeping us from reaching our full potential?

7 RESOURCES
What are our greatest resources?

8 QUARTERLY PRIORITIES
In the next 90 days, what are our specific, measurable, targets of accomplishments?

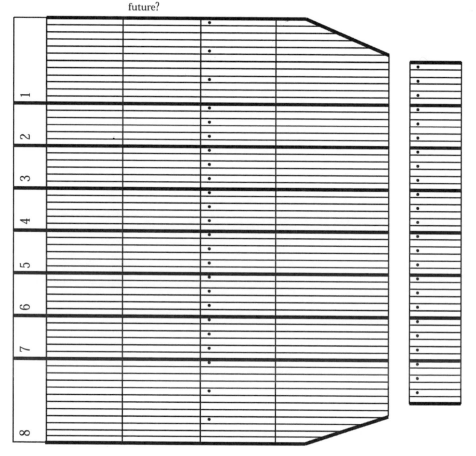

Your name _____ Date _____ Organization_____

Division _____ Dept. _____Section _____ Program _____

18

"You ought to say, 'If it is the Lord's will, we will live and do this or that." James 4:15 (NIV)

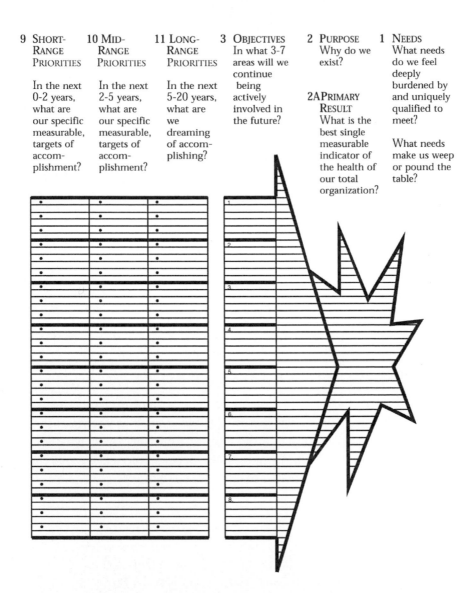

9 SHORT-RANGE PRIORITIES

In the next 0-2 years, what are our specific measurable, targets of accomplishment?

10 MID-RANGE PRIORITIES

In the next 2-5 years, what are our specific measurable, targets of accomplishment?

11 LONG-RANGE PRIORITIES

In the next 5-20 years, what are we dreaming of accomplishing?

3 OBJECTIVES
In what 3-7 areas will we continue being actively involved in the future?

2 PURPOSE
Why do we exist?

2A PRIMARY RESULT
What is the best single measurable indicator of the health of our total organization?

1 NEEDS
What needs do we feel deeply burdened by and uniquely qualified to meet?

What needs make us weep or pound the table?

This is a simplified representation of the 24" x 36" Strategic Planning Arrow. To order the actual **Strategic Planning Arrow** for your church or organization, please visit BobbBiehl.com or call 1-800-443-1976.

Chapter Overview

- Frequent Elephant Stakes
- Tool One: The Strategic Planning Arrow
- A Quick Overview of a Strategic Planning Arrow

Frequent Elephant Stakes

Beware of these elephant stakes that prevent you from developing a Strategic Plan:

- "Strategic Planning is so complicated, I don't even know where to start."

  Start with direction.

- "I don't know what goes into an organizational Strategic Plan."

  The DOCTOR components make up a Strategic Plan.

- "A Strategic Plan just sits in a notebook on the shelf and gathers dust. Why bother?"

  Without setting up your tracking, evaluation, and refinement, it will sit on a shelf; however, once you set up those three, it will continue to be a dynamic tool in your leadership process.

Tool One: *The Strategic Planning Arrow*

In 1980, I was assigned the task of leading a planning exercise for the Focus on the Family board. Around two o'clock in the morning, an idea crystallized. If we had a big enough sheet of paper, we could get our whole direction on a single sheet. I began sketching and the Strategic Planning Arrow began to take shape. Since that time, more than 30,000 people have ordered Strategic Planning Arrows and worked through this planning exercise.

The Strategic Planning Arrow Provides a Crystal-Clear Track to Run On
Track + Action =Traction

Many people develop a beautiful plan. They have a detailed track laid out for the next 10 years, but they take no action. Others *do* a lot, but have no clear plan. When you combine a clear plan with action, you get traction. You begin moving from where you are to where you want to go.

THE STRATEGIC PLANNING ARROW
DEVELOPS "STRATEGIC ARROW LOGIC"

Since 1980, many young leaders have come up to me and said: "You know, Bobb, even when I don't have a Strategic Planning Arrow handy, I'm using Strategic Arrow logic. Whenever I'm given a project, I begin asking myself: 'What are the needs of this project? Why are we doing this? What are our basic objectives?'" When you learn to use a Strategic Planning Arrow, you will find your mind has been trained to think logically and sequentially.

THE STRATEGIC PLANNING ARROW IS
ALWAYS DEVELOPED SEQUENTIALLY

Part of the reason the Arrow process is so helpful is that it is sequential. Regardless of the organization or situation, the place you start is always the same, and the next steps in the process are always the same.

An old expression holds that "a cat always lands on its feet." I once saw a television commercial in which a cat was dropped out of a window while its reaction were filmed in slow motion. The cat was held on its back, with its feet in the air, and then dropped. As the cat fell, the first thing it did was to get its head straight. The cat turned just its head, leaving its feet pointing up, and looked at the ground. Once the cat knew where the ground was, it turned its body so that it landed feet first.

If you serve on a board, lead an organization, or pastor a church, you always need to be able to get your head straight and land on your feet. To do that, follow a systematic, step-by-step process. No matter what you are asked to plan, you always start at the same point: "What needs are we trying to meet? What needs do we feel deeply burdened by and uniquely qualified to meet?" Need or greed is the starting point of most planning. When the needs are identified, then you ask, "Why does our organization exist?"

Once you understand the Strategic Planning Arrow at its essential level, you can land on your feet as a leader anywhere, at anytime, for the rest of your life.

THE STRATEGIC PLANNING ARROW WORKS FOR A "MOM-AND-POP" BUSINESS OR A MAJOR CORPORATION

This planning process is highly adaptable and extremely flexible. It can be used in a wide variety of situations, from small "mom-and-pop" businesses to major corporations. The Strategic Planning Arrow identifies the key ingredients of planning at any level.

THE STRATEGIC PLANNING ARROW IS A LIFELONG TOOL

No matter what you are asked to plan, no matter where you go or what you do, for the rest of your life you can use the Strategic Planning Arrow as a tool to begin clarifying your team's direction. And it is available twenty-four hours a day, seven days a week—whenever you need it! The Strategic Planning Arrow gives you a way to refocus your thinking at any time in the future.

YOU *NEVER* HAVE TO START OVER

Many years ago, sitting on a park bench in South Bend, Indiana, I thought, *Well, I should start setting some priorities.* I found an envelope and wrote my priorities on the back of it. Three years later I found that envelope—in the bottom of a drawer.

How many times have you put together a plan, and then forgotten it? You felt like you'd never had a plan, like you were as foggy as you'd ever been, right?

Once you complete a Strategic Planning Arrow, the furthest you will ever be from crystal-clear focus is probably about 10 to 30 minutes. You simply get out your Strategic Planning Arrow and reassess: "Are these still the needs we care deeply about? Is this still our purpose? Are these still our objectives?" Work back through the Arrow and refine what you wrote in the past. You will probably find that you are more in focus than you thought you were. You never have to start over once you get "draft one" done. You just improve it. You don't have to recreate the wheel; you just keep refining the tire.

THE STRATEGIC PLANNING ARROW
CAN HELP IN THE FUND-RAISING PROCESS

Without a clear plan, fund-raising is more difficult. People rarely give money if there isn't a clear vision. Let me tell you a true story. I got a call one day from Rudy Howard, an inner-city director of Young Life's Urban Program in Houston. He said, "Brother Bobb, I just called to bless your heart." I said, "Great, Rudy! Tell me what's up." He said, "Remember you told us to get out the Strategic Planning Arrow when we were going to make a financial request from someone? You told us to tell them what the needs were and start weeping and pounding the table about the needs. Then tell them why our team is here and tell them what we're going to do about the need. Tell them what we've already done about it and what we want to do about it.

"Well, I went to this foundation and I told them what the needs of the Houston inner-city kids were. I told them some stories about those kids, and I started to cry, and I started to pound the table. I told them why we're here. I did just exactly what you told me. At the end of that time, they said, 'Brother Rudy, would you mind waiting in the outer office while we discuss this?' My heart sank because I thought they were going to say, 'Well, not this year, Rudy.'

"They called me back into the room. You won't believe it. They told me, 'Rudy, you've asked for $5000. We're not going to give you $5000.' My heart sank even lower. They said, 'We're going to give you $10,000. We have never seen a clearer presentation of what someone planned to do in the inner city of Houston. We're going to give you $10,000, and if you'll just keep us up-to-date, you can come back, and we'll give you some more as you need it.'"

This is what frequently comes from having a crystal-clear plan. People get excited when they see needs and know you have a clear plan to meet those needs and care deeply about meeting them.

A Quick Overview of a Strategic Planning Arrow

Take a few minutes and get familiar with the Strategic Planning Arrow (see pages 18-19). Study the terms and steps of the Arrow process.

Welcome back. At the top right side of the Strategic Planning Arrow, you will see a Scripture verse, James 4:15 (NIV). It says, "You ought to say, 'If it is the Lord's will, we will live and do this or that.'" As a young leader, I wrestled with knowing whether or not a Christian should try to plan future direction. James says in 4:14, "Why, you do not even know what will happen tomorrow. What is your life? You are a mist that appears for a little while and then vanishes." I thought perhaps that meant that we shouldn't make plans for the future. Other people have also stopped there and said, "Well, why plan? We are just a mist, and we are going to vanish anyway."

Go on and read verse 15: "Instead, you *ought* [this is a command or a directive] to say, 'If it is the Lord's will, we will live and do this or that'" (emphasis mine). It isn't a matter of whether or not we should make plans, it's a matter of our attitude when making the plans. It is sinful to say, "This is what we will do, regardless of what God wants." We should say, *"If it is the Lord's will*, we will…do this or that." (Italics added.)

During planning, stop and pray at different points in the process. Ask, "Is this Your will, Father?" Commit the whole planning process to prayer and say, "God, we are seeking Your will, not our will. It isn't what we want to do, but what You want us to do that is important to us."

In the Strategic Planning Arrow you'll see some numbers. At the top of the arrow (the right of the page), it says, "1—Needs." Then, if you move to the left, "2—Purpose" and "3—Objectives." These numbers represent the *sequence* with which you should define any team's direction. (Each step is developed in detail in following chapters.)

The *first* thing you need to do is ask the following: "What needs do we feel deeply burdened by and uniquely qualified to meet? What needs make us weep or pound the table?"

Second, you ask, "In light of these needs, why do we, as an organization, exist?"

Third, "In what three to seven areas will we continue being actively involved in the future?" In other words, what must we continue doing if we are to meet the needs we have identified and fulfill the purpose we have defined? What categories of activity are we going to be involved in over the next few years? Examples for churches are: worship and music, Christian education, pastoral care, or missions.

These first three steps (needs, purpose, and objectives) give you a *focus* for any organization, and they tend to stay the same over the years. The kinds of needs your organization is meeting today (e.g., caring for unwed mothers) are likely the same kinds of needs it was meeting 10 years ago. They may differ a little bit. The demographics of your area may change. The needs of the people you serve may change. Your heart motivation may mature or change. But basically the needs that motivate your organization, its purpose, and its objectives will be similar to what they were 10 years ago and what they will be 10 years from now.

Once you have completed these three steps you will have a sense of focus. If you, the board, and your staff are in agreement on needs, purpose, and objectives, there will be a sense of unity in the organization. "Here are the needs we are meeting. Here's why we exist. Here's what we are going to do about it!"

Fourth, move your eye to the bottom of the Arrow (far left on the page) where it says, "4—Milestones." In each of the objective areas you will ask yourself, "What major milestones have we already accomplished?"

Fifth, in each objective area, ask the question, "What ideas do we have that we could consider turning into priorities in the future?" In other words, don't ever lose a good idea.

Sixth, in each objective area, ask, "What roadblocks are keeping us from reaching our full potential?" List only the top three roadblocks in each area.

Seventh, in each objective area, ask: "What resources are available to help meet the needs we identified and overcome our roadblocks?" List only the top three.

Eighth, in each objective area, ask, "If we could only do three measurable things in the next 90 days to meet the needs we care about, what would we do? In the next 90 days, what are our specific, measurable targets of accomplishment?"

Ninth, in each objective area, ask, "What are our specific, measurable targets of accomplishment in the next two years?" These are your short-range priorities.

Tenth, in each objective area, ask, "What are our specific, measurable targets of accomplishment in the next two to five years?" These are your mid-range priorities.

Eleventh, in each objective area, ask, "What are our specific, measurable targets of accomplishment in the next five to 20 years?" These are your long-range priorities.

This brief overview gives you a general feeling of the Strategic Planning Arrow process—the eleven steps to a crystal-clear direction.

One of the advantages of having the Strategic Planning Arrow on one large piece of paper (for ordering information, see page 17) is that everyone on your board and each of your staff members can begin to see how all the pieces fit together. Everyone can see how her/his part of the organization fits into the big picture.

You've probably experienced the frustration of dealing with a staff member who is passionate about her/his area of responsibility and seems to assume that all of the budget should go to her/his area. We want staff members who are passionate about their area, and it's normal to want the biggest piece of the pie for one's own department. All staff members, however, must see their projects in the context of the needs of the whole organization. With the whole team's priorities on a single piece of paper, you have a context in which to appreciate the proper distribution of available resources. Each staff member can see the need to work in harmony and balance with the other staff members. That's when your organization begins functioning as a team.

You now have a quick overview of a Strategic Planning Arrow. Now let's go through the Arrow on a step-by-step basis starting at square one—needs.

PART TWO

The Strategic Planning Arrow

CHAPTER 4

Arrow Step One: Needs

Chapter Overview

- Understanding Needs
- Key Questions to Help You Define the Needs You Will Address
- Needs Are the Father of Creativity Just as Necessity Is the Mother of Invention

> **The Strategic Planning process begins with a simple, yet profound, question:**
>
> What needs do we feel deeply burdened by and uniquely qualified to meet?

Understanding Needs

In order to effectively plan for the future you need to understand what *needs* are and why it is important to identify them.

NEEDS ARE CATEGORICALLY SPECIFIC

The needs you list are *categories* in that they can include thousands of people, but at the same time they are very defined and specific. For example, the needs we feel deeply burdened by and uniquely qualified to meet might be: homes for unwed mothers, troops for Boy/Girl Scouts, retirement housing, and so forth. In a for-profit corporation, these needs would be major needs in the market.

NEEDS SHOULD MAKE US FEEL EMOTIONAL

Determining needs involves the "feeling" side of planning. Ask yourself, "What makes me weep or pound the table?"

You may say, "Bobb, I'm just not an emotional person. I don't weep and pound the table about anything." Well then, what issues deeply concern you? To what cause would you donate money?

Typically, the first responses we hear from clients to this question are related to needs within the organization. "We need more office space," or "We need three new staff members." Needs inside the organization should be listed under roadblocks on your Strategic Planning Arrow, not in the needs section. Any organization, church, or business that is focused on meeting its own needs first will soon quit growing and die.

Ask yourself, "If Jesus were alive—in person and bodily form—in my community, what would make Him weep or pound the table? What would make Him weep as He did as He looked over Jerusalem, or what would make Him turn the tables like He did with the money changers?" What would make Jesus weep or pound the table if He were part of your community? These things are precisely what should make us weep and pound the table!

NEEDS ARE THE STARTING POINT OF THE PLANNING PROCESS

One client said it best when he said, "When we clearly defined the needs our team would meet, it was like the entire planning process moved from boring black-and-white to exciting living color. Before we carefully analyzed the needs, planning was just a dull exercise, something we needed to do annually. But once we began to see the needs of children without fathers, broken homes, widows, orphans, single parents, teenagers with drug problems, unwed mothers, and the other needs right in our own community, planning suddenly became far more meaningful to us. Planning a youth facility or a home for unwed mothers became very exciting!"

You must invest what might seem to be a disproportionate amount of your time making certain that your team agrees upon which needs you will meet. Seeing and feeling needs deeply moves your plan in the minds of board members from "your ego trip" to "what we must do!"

Key Questions to Help You Define the Needs You Will Address

WHO ARE THE PEOPLE WE SERVE?

Frequently a planning team will ask one of our consultants, "We are concerned about a lot of things. How do we distinguish between those needs that we should commit to meeting and those we shouldn't?" That's why the second part of the question is important: what needs are you uniquely qualified to meet? Are you deeply concerned about this need *and* uniquely qualified to meet it?

You and your organization are not equipped or qualified to meet all of the needs in your area of influence. You are equipped to meet *some of the needs* in your community. Identify those. Conversely, *you* and *your organization* are equipped to meet some of the needs in your community. You may feel that a national organization could do more, or that a particular famous leader could do better meeting this need than you could. That may be true, but they haven't been placed in this community. You have.

WHAT IS THE MOST URGENT NEED IN OUR COMMUNITY TODAY?

What are the most urgent needs our team might address? The following is a list of things most of our children will face before they reach the age of 50. They will see these issues on television, experience them, or be affected by them before leaving home.

AIDS

Alcoholism

Assassinations

Bankruptcy

Birth defects

Change—at a mind-shocking rate

Computerization—exponential separation of computer literates/
  illiterates

Cost of living—making housing costs prohibitive

Crime and violence—urban and rural

Date rape

Death

Depression

Disease

Divorce

Drugs and drug-related crimes/pressure

Earthquakes

Educational values corrosion

Environmental pollution

Failure

Family breakdown

Financial pressure

Futility

Gangs—threat/pressure

Governmental corruption

Homeless population explosion

Homosexual pressure groups

Individuals with disabilities

International threats and turbulence

Position loss and/or constant occupational change

Legal problems—immoral laws/lawsuits

Medical problems—security-threatening bills
Mental illness
Midlife crisis
Military draft potential
Mobility breaking apart the fabric of our families
Movies—thousands of movies watched by the age of 10 (many violent)
Murder—commonplace; drive-by shootings
Newspapers—thousands of pages per day available
Pornography—soft-and hard-core
Prison—criminal; political
Rape
Recession/depression
Rejection
Relativism—"no absolutes"
Rewritten history—where it is hard to believe anything
Riots
Sexual perversion
Sexually transmitted diseases
Space travel
Spin masters reinterpreting all of life
Substance abuse
Suicide
Tax burden
Tax audit trauma
Television—24 hours; a myriad of channels; live wars
Terrorists—local; international
Unemployment
Urban blight
War
World hunger

These are just a few we could name. Which ones will we want to help them cure? If we don't meet these needs, who will? If not now, when?

When George Romney was the governor of Michigan, he made a statement that caught my attention as a young student at Michigan State University. After giving the audience a grand challenge, he exhorted us, "Ask yourself these two questions, 'If not now, when? If not me, who?'" As you look at the needs around you, ask yourself and your team those two questions.

Needs Are the Father of Creativity
Just as Necessity Is the Mother of Invention

Over the years I have developed many programs or materials that have caused people to say, "What a creative idea! What a unique idea!" One day I sat down and reflected on the question, "Where did these ideas come from?" Do you know what I determined? The common denominator of every original idea I've had in my life was a deep concern and desire for action about a need. I didn't know what to do, and I'd never seen anyone do it! I thought, *Just because no one has done it doesn't mean someone shouldn't do it. Therefore, I'll try it!*

When you and your team begin looking at needs, it will spark creative thinking. When you meet eye-to-eye with someone with dramatic needs, you will begin to generate new ideas to help them.

As you identify the needs you care about deeply and are uniquely qualified to meet, paint word pictures of the needs to your board, your staff, and your constituents in "living color." The more "living color," the stronger your emotional motivation to meet those needs. Think of a person who vividly represents each of the needs. One way to add "color" is to put a person's first name by each need on your Arrow.

Personalizing the areas of need will remind you that the needs identified on your Strategic Planning Arrow are more than concepts and noble intentions. These are flesh-and-blood people. They are fellow human beings with deep personal needs, people you can touch, help, hug, encourage! If someone tried to convince you that this wasn't a real need, you would become emotional. You would say, "Something *has* to be done for these people!" You'd remember that poor little girl who was pregnant and didn't know what to do. You might begin to cry. Attaching the name of a person you've encountered will personalize the area of need.

Assignment:

Your first assignment is to list 10 to 15 specific needs you feel deeply interested in/concerned about and uniquely qualified to meet. Place a person's first name by each need to make it personally meaningful to you.

1.

2.

3.

4.

5.

6.

7.

8.

9.

10.

11.

12.

13.

14.

15.

Welcome back. The next step in the planning process is to define your purpose.

CHAPTER 5

Arrow Step Two: Purpose

Chapter Overview

- How to Write Your Purpose Statement
- Key Questions to Help Clarify Your Purpose
- A Few Sample Purpose Statements
- Additional Benefits of a Purpose Statement

Note: A "purpose statement" is also sometimes called a "mission statement." Our firm uses "purpose statement" in a church setting because of the potential to confuse "mission statement" with missions work. In business, using the term "mission statement" is not a problem.

> **In light of the needs discussed previously, the next question to ask is:**
>
> Why does our team exist?

How to Write Your Purpose Statement

The process of finalizing your team's purpose statement with your board and your staff may require several hours and several drafts. I have consulted with groups that took a full day just to define a one-sentence purpose statement. They hammered, chipped, and chiseled away until everyone in the room felt 100 percent comfortable with every word. However long it takes, stay with the task. It is a critical piece of your organization's direction.

So How Do You Go About Defining A Purpose Statement?

❏ 1. Write Any Way You Like Using as Many Words as You Like

Your first task is to identify all the components you might want in your purpose statement. Imagine a person asking you why your organization exists. What would you say? If s/he thought about your answer, then asked, "Why is that important?" what would you say next? If s/he insisted on probing further and further, asking again and again, "Why is that important?" what layers of purpose and meaning would reveal themselves? Take fifteen pages, if you need to, to answer the question, "Why does our team exist?"

❏ 2. Now Use the Opposite Approach—Use a Single Word to Express the Focus of Why You Exist

One exercise that will be very meaningful to your team is to ask, "What single word is the bull's-eye of the bull's-eye, the focus of the focus, the center of the center, the very essence of our organization?" This word is not your purpose statement, but it is the single-word focus for your organization. Come to agreement on this single-word focus as a leadership team.

I sat down one night with the board of a church of about four thousand people and we started the process of finding a single word that would express the focus of their church. It ended up taking us an hour and a half, which surprised me.

People said, "Well, I think the focus of our church is missions." Others said, "I think it's evangelism." Another said, "I think it's serving." "I think it's meeting needs." "I think it's Christian education." "I think it's... " We came up with 54 word possibilities. Then we said, "All right, some of these overlap. Let's try to get it down to 25." So some we combined, some we eliminated. We got it down to 18. Then we got it down to six, and then three, and finally one.

Before I tell you what that one word was, I'd like to suggest that you put this book down right now and take as much time as it requires to come to your own team's single-word focus. What is the one word that brings focus to every meeting your team has, every seminar you sponsor, every community outreach, every program, every thing you do? What is the internal core, the essence, the single word that brings meaning to everything you do?

Our single word focus is _____.

Welcome back. The word that we came to that night was "Jesus." The single reason for the church is not a program, not a principle, not a process. It's a person. It's Jesus Christ.

❐ 3. Write One Non-Technical Sentence.

The next step is to say, "Instead of having one word, I have three words, 'Jesus _____?'" What would be the three words that you would use to define or begin focusing the energies of your team?

_____

_____

_____

Now try to put that three-word phrase into one non-technical sentence that anyone can understand. I call this "party conversation." If you went to a mayor's reception, and the mayor asked what your team is all about, what would you say? Refine your purpose statement so you could readily and simply say, "Mr. Mayor, the reason we exist is to…"

Masterplanning Group's purpose statement is, *"Strengthening Christian leaders."* That's why we exist. That's what I tell people at parties. That's what I tell people on airplanes. That's why our entire firm exists. Everything we do is to maximize your leadership ability, to put resources in your hand and in your mind that can maximize your ability to lead people as a Christian. That's simple. That's clear. That's party-level communication.

Key Questions to Help Clarify Your Purpose

As you develop your purpose statement it will help to ask yourself a few key questions.

HOW ARE WE UNIQUE FROM ANY OTHER GROUP OR ORGANIZATION?

If you are part of a national organization, denomination, or corporation, your purpose statement is frequently the purpose statement for the larger group but modified for a local area. You are simply carrying out that same purpose in a given geographic area. Your uniqueness from another team down the street under the same national name may be only geographic. On the other hand, your team or organization may be the only one of its kind in the world. Whatever your degree of uniqueness, define that for yourself.

WHAT WOULD WE WANT OUR TEAM'S EPITAPH TO BE?

An epitaph is a past-tense purpose statement. Think about your own life for a minute. What would you like your epitaph to say? As a matter of fact, if you've never thought about it, why don't you set this book aside for a few minutes and think about this question. What would you like chiseled in granite on your grave marker?

Dr. Frank Laubauch's epitaph reads, "He taught the world to read." During his life, his purpose statement would have been, "To teach the world to read." See the connection? A good way to examine what we are doing in life is to decide what we would like our epitaph to be when we are done with life. It's a different approach that sometimes brings surprising clarity.

Assignment:

Write your team's epitaph—a past-tense purpose statement. What would you like your team's epitaph to read?

Now put this book down and take as long as you need to come to a crystal-clear, one-sentence statement of why your team exists. Write a statement with which your team can agree 100 percent.

Our team exists to:

_____

To get you started it may be helpful to see others' purpose statements. (You can also find 10 other easily adaptable sample purpose statements for your team to review in Appendix A-3.)

Sample Purpose Statements

Masterplanning Group International:

"Strengthening the Christian leaders."

Evangelism Explosion International:

"To glorify God by equipping the body of Christ worldwide for friendship, evangelism, discipleship, and healthy growth."

Evangelical United Brethren's "epitaph":

"These people communicated the Gospel of Christ by word and deed and taught all men and women how to be saved and become faithful disciples of Christ and responsible members of His Church."

Evangelical United Brethren denomination's purpose statement:

"To effectively communicate the Gospel by word and deed toward the end that all men and women shall be saved and become faithful disciples of Christ and responsible members of His Church."

(Local churches can adopt the denominational purpose by including the name of the local church and the local city or town. Likewise, pastors or church members can personalize their church's purpose statement as their own.)

One Evangelical United Brethren local church's purpose statement:

"By the enabling grace of God to glorify God with a lifestyle of worshiping His Name, nurturing people, and sharing His Gospel with the community and the world."

One independent church's purpose statement:

> *"To present Christ in a contemporary, creative, credible, and caring way to all people in an environment where people from the community and the world can trust Christ and grow to their full potential in Him."*

Christ Community Church in Omaha:

> *"To make disciples of Jesus Christ by winning people to faith in Christ, building them in the Word of Christ, and equipping them to fulfill the Great Commission of Christ."*

Welcome back. How does it feel to have a crystal-clear purpose statement?

Additional Benefits of a Purpose Statement

Before we move on to the third step of our process, "Objectives," here are a few additional benefits of having a clear purpose statement:

A CLEARLY DEFINED PURPOSE STATEMENT Is Very Freeing

Investing the time in identifying your purpose as a team is a freeing process. It begins with some difficulty, confusion, differing opinions, and clarifying discussions; but the end result is freedom! Excitement! It is not unlike the sensation backpackers feel when they complete an arduous trek up the trail to the crest of the mountain. They can see for miles. The trail is clear before them. They know where to go next. They have a proper perspective.

Having a clear purpose statement also helps you determine which things you *do not* need to do, which is also very freeing!

A CLEARLY DEFINED PURPOSE STATEMENT Helps Focus Activity

Any church, organization, or business is a collection of individuals who have their own assumptions about *what* should be done and *why*. A clear purpose statement helps channel all this individual effort toward one single purpose and direction. This is the beauty of a purpose statement. It says, "This is why we work so hard as a team."

A CLEARLY DEFINED PURPOSE STATEMENT
Is Easy for a Team to Memorize

Dr. Gordon McDonald, former senior pastor of the Lexington Chapel in Concord, Massachusetts, helped focus the church by asking the whole congregation to memorize their purpose statement. It was a simple statement of why their church existed—a statement they could tell a friend at a party. He had them recite it week after week as a congregation. In a short time, every member of the entire church could tell you precisely why they existed as a church in their community. It was a good way to transfer organizational focus from the leadership team to the whole congregation.

A CLEARLY DEFINED PURPOSE STATEMENT
Gives You a Clear, Consistent Sense of Direction

Now you're clear why your team exists. You have a clear purpose statement. You have a team North Star. The North Star is not a destination but a directional indicator, like a compass. It is not where we end up, but the direction in which we keep heading. When you reel out of a complex and overwhelming meeting asking, "What was that budget figure again, where are we, where are we going, and why are we here?" you can always come back to your purpose and say, "Oh yes, we're not just here to manage budgets. We're here to: 'Make disciples of Jesus Christ by winning people to faith in Christ, building them in the Word of Christ, and equipping them to fulfill the Great Commission of Christ.'" Your purpose statement gives you perspective on why you are doing everything you are doing.

CHAPTER 6

Arrow Step Three: Objectives

Chapter Overview

- Defining Your Planning Terms
- Organizing Your Objectives
- It's Time to Pray

Objectives identify the things we will do to meet the needs we have identified and to fulfill the purpose we have defined.

Objectives answer the question:

In what three to seven areas will we continue
being actively involved in the future?

Today's leadership vocabulary contains words that mean different things to different people. If you ask a group of 50 people to define *leadership* you may get 49 different definitions. The same is true with the word *success*. Today there is no unanimously accepted or understood definition of the word *success*. Another set of words used by people to mean very different things is *purpose, objectives,* and *priorities.*

Defining Your Planning Terms

Defining these three words is important because members of most boards come from all walks of life. They are more like an All-Star team (the best and the brightest from industry, business, education, etc.) than a Super Bowl team (an experienced, functioning unit that has played together for years, and who work with great precision). In the huddle, the quarterback on the All-Star team says, "Okay, red rooster over two." But to one player "red rooster" means an end run, to another player it means a quarterback sneak, and to another it means punt! Like an All-Star team, the board comes together once a week for an hour or so, and occasionally at retreats. They try to communicate, plan, and make decisions, but they sometimes use different words to mean the same thing.

If an All-Star team is to play together, they have to agree on the meanings of terms used to play. The same is true for your board and team members. An engineer will use the word *goal* to mean a clearly defined, measurable target of achievement, and *objectives* to mean broad statements of focused energy and resources. An educator will use the words in exactly the opposite manner. Expressions used at individual workplaces may be different, but on the board and across your team you need to use agreed-upon terms and definitions.

A common language makes it easier to communicate clearly and plan effectively, and it helps build a sense of team spirit, both locally and nationally. If you belong to a nationwide or international organization, it is highly beneficial for all team members to agree on the meaning of planning terms. If a team member moves to another church or office within the organization, communicating vision and priorities will be less confusing.

When I first started trying to define the terms *purpose, objectives,* and *priorities* (goals or problems), I had been consulting for about four years. As a lecturer, consultant, and team leader, I didn't understand the terms myself. I began reading and asking people, "How do you define these terms?" You know what? I heard so much confusion, I couldn't believe it. Over the years I have developed simple definitions that team members tend to agree upon quickly regardless of their individual backgrounds. If these planning terms and definitions make sense to you, consider using them with your entire team:

	Purpose	Objectives	Priorities
Definition	A single statement of why something or someone exists.	General areas in which effort is directed.	A specific plan to achieve a measurable result within a specific amount of time.
Questions Answered	*Why?* Why do I exist?	*What generally?* In what six to 10 areas will I continue being actively involved in the future?	*What specifically?* What *specific* things will I do to move in the direction of my purpose and objectives?
Characteristics	Written: *non-measurable*, non-dated, one sentence	Written: six to 10 areas: *non-measurable*, non-dated	Written: three to 24 per year: *measurable*, time-dated
Could be introduced by the phrase	The reason I exist is to...	Over the next five to 20 years I want to continue...	During the next 12 months I plan to...
Amount of time the statement can be expected to last without revision	Twenty years to a lifetime	One to 10 years	Short-, Mid,- Long-term priorities.
Example	Our church exists to bring people into a mature relationship with God.	Provide Christian education for our church.	Recruit ten new teachers for Sunday school by November 1.

You may find these examples of typical church-department objectives (listed alphabetically) helpful:

Sample Objective Statements

ADMINISTRATIVE SERVICES

Provide administrative support of church ministries with appropriate quality, effectiveness, and efficiency while being excellent stewards of people, property, and finances.

CHRISTIAN EDUCATION

Help those involved find a caring community, establish a meaningful place of service, trust the Lord Jesus as their Savior, and begin the process of trusting Him in their everyday life.

COMMUNICATION SERVICES

Communicate the life of the congregation to the congregation and to our whole community.

MISSIONS (HOME AND FOREIGN) AND OUTREACH (EVANGELISM)

Equip members to reach out to their community and the world with the gospel of Christ.

PASTORAL CARE

Equip people with a biblical model so they can assist those in the church community to handle life's struggles with maturity and to become obedient disciples reaching out to others.

SCHOOL

Train students to be disciples of Jesus Christ in all aspects of their lives.

WORSHIP AND MUSIC

Bring people to a vital worship of the one true God.

Organizing Your Objectives

Our firm has worked with a variety of organizational structures that help clarify objectives. Let me illustrate the wide variety of ways to organize a team by illustrating how it can work in one local church.

ORGANIZATIONAL OBJECTIVES CAN BE ORGANIZED FUNCTIONALLY

You can organize your team planning around the various functions of a church. For example: worship and music, Christian education, pastoral care, outreach, missions, and so forth. At the local church level, one of the most effective organizational charts is a functional division of labor.

ORGANIZATIONAL OBJECTIVES CAN BE ORGANIZED BY AGE OR MARKET

You can organize your church planning around everything you do with preschool, elementary, junior high, high school, college/career, young adults, middle age, senior adults, and so forth.

ORGANIZATIONAL OBJECTIVES CAN BE ORGANIZED GEOGRAPHICALLY

You could divide your ministry objectives by geographic regions. In some companies it's better to break it up that way. This may not be true at the local church level but at the national level, such as a denomination, you may use a geographic division to define objective areas—"You are responsible for the Eastern region; you are responsible for the Midwestern region; you are responsible for the Western region."

One of the best ways to tell whether or not an objective area is clearly defined is to ask, "Could I assign a person to be responsible for this objective area?" For example, could I ask a person to be responsible for all of Christian education? The answer is yes. To be responsible for all of missions? Yes. If an objective area is not clearly defined, perhaps you need to reorganize your objectives.

Assignment:

Create a first draft of your team's objective areas. Briefly define why that objective area exists. The above objectives will work as a model for many churches (additional samples of objectives are in Appendix A-6). Feel free to adapt these to your use.

After you've finished, take a break and then make sure your needs, purpose, and objectives are clearly stated.

Now that you have identified the needs you want to address, defined your purpose, and determined your objectives, you have a sense of focus.

- These are needs we are meeting.
- This is why we are committed to meeting these needs.
- This is what we are going to do about these needs.

The first three steps provide a focus that won't change much over the next five to 10 years. Review them annually to make sure they are still relevant.

It's Time to Pray

Before we move on to Step 4—Milestones—you can see that there is a break in the Arrow. There is a white line down the middle that separates what could be called the "arrowhead" from the "shaft" of the arrow. May I suggest that you write a word in that white area vertically? Write the word *prayer*.

Pause at this point to ask God to continue to help you care about those things for which He cares. First, that you would see the needs God sees. Second, that you would truly understand God's purpose for your team. Third, that He would work through you to move in the direction of the objectives you've defined.

CHAPTER 7

Arrow Step Four: Milestones

Chapter Overview

- From Objectives to Milestones
- Writing Down Your Milestones

After you have established your objectives, ask yourselves:
What major milestones have we already accomplished?

From Objectives to Milestones

For each of your objective areas, work through the rest of the Arrow steps. Let's use Christian education as an example. Go to the "Christian education" band on the Arrow and move across to the left side. There you will see a white area. You can write "Christian education" in there as well so that when you are working with the whole Strategic Planning Arrow, you don't have to keep looking back to the objectives to see which band is which. Begin working your way back to the right on the Arrow, completing the remaining steps of the Arrow process. "Milestones" is the next step after needs, purpose, and objectives.

Milestones Are Transitional

You were headed in one direction, and you moved in a whole different way—a major milestone! You brought in a new curriculum—a major milestone! You got a new Christian education director—a major milestone! You built new office space—a major milestone! You hosted a national conference—a major milestone! You initiated a teacher training program—a major milestone! What are the milestones that you have already accomplished?

Milestones Are Measurable and Typically Dated for Future Record

Measurability can be by date or by amount. You can say, "On January 1, 2020, we moved into our new sanctuary." That is measurable. Or, you can simply say, "We moved into our new sanctuary." Your whole team knows exactly what and when you mean.

Milestones Instill Confidence

It is not uncommon for team leaders (I use the term *team leader* to mean boss, manager, foreman, team leader, etc.) to get discouraged. They come to the end of a year and can't identify any significant progress during that year. They often can't remember any tangible results. Most of their accomplishments are intangible. Changed lives tend to melt into the daily activity of living.

I talk with many leaders who say things like, "This year I stayed up late a lot of nights. I got up early every morning. I gave a lot of talks. I helped a lot of friends. I helped a lot of families in trouble. I did all kinds of things. But do you know what? At the end of the year, I don't have a single book that I've written, or building that I've built, or car that I've manufactured. I don't have anything tangible that says I, as a leader, was here this year. All I can say is that I was doing what I was supposed to be doing this year." We tend *not* to give trophies to leaders for having another outstanding year.

On the Strategic Planning Arrow, team leaders are asked to write down the major, tangible progress made by the team. When team leaders get discouraged (I've done this myself), they can look back at the milestones and say, "Hey, wait a minute. We've come a long way here!" It's like a pocketful of sunshine for a rainy day.

Whenever I get discouraged, I tend to look at two things: the milestones of the past and the priorities for the future. My wife Cheryl and I talk a fair amount about the fact that life has a lot of depressing things—responsibilities, burdens, disappointments. Using a fishing analogy, these heavy pressures are like sinkers weighing us down. What we need are a few bobbers in life that keep bringing us to the top. Milestones are like bobbers. They help you look back and celebrate. "Hey, you know, we really did accomplish more than it seemed this year!"

MILESTONES PROVIDE A BASIS FOR FUTURE PLANNING

When we want to plan priorities for the future, it is difficult if we don't know what our past has been. It's difficult to know what our budget should be if we don't know what our budget was last year. Having milestones written down—"We had a record budget of $483 thousand this year"—gives us a context for planning next year's budget.

MILESTONES HELP WHEN ORIENTING NEW STAFF

Writing down your milestones is like recording history a little bit at a time. When a new team member joins your team, you need to orient them. Showing them the milestones helps them understand your history and consequently, your culture, your mode of doing business, your progress, your heart. You can say, "Here are the needs we see. Here is our purpose. Here are our objective areas. Here are some of our recent milestones."

When your Milestone section gets full, start keeping a file called, "History." Keep a list for each year. Keep this record year after year to remind yourself of your organization's turning points.

Writing Down Your Milestones

Listing milestones instills the team with confidence. If you haven't yet filled out your milestones, do so now. Discussing needs, purpose, and objectives can be heavy, even uncomfortable. Milestones allow you to celebrate! Write down milestones for each objective area.

Objective:_____   Objective:_____

Milestones:_____   Milestones:_____

_____   _____

_____   _____

_____   _____

Objective:_____   Objective:_____

Milestones:_____   Milestones:_____

_____   _____

_____   _____

_____   _____

CHAPTER 8

Arrow Step Five: Ideas

Chapter Overview

- Never Lose a Great Idea
- Time Is Money; Ideas Are Also Money
- File Backup

Milestones celebrate past accomplishments. Successful organizations celebrate the past while keeping a sharp focus on the future.

They ask:
What ideas have we had that we should consider turning into priorities?

Never Lose a Great Idea

Have you ever had a conversation similar to this:

Other person: Hey, did you hear about this idea that just made 43 zillion dollars?

You: You know, I thought of that idea a few years ago.

Other person: Well, why didn't you do something about it?

You: (Sheepishly) Well, I sort of forgot that I ever thought about it.

Many great ideas are lost to history, lost in our minds. Never lose a good idea!

One day I asked myself, "What gives a person a feeling of 'I am organized'?" I eventually concluded that my grandmother, Cora Donaldson, was right when she said, "Have a place for everything, and everything in its place." When we have a place for everything, and everything is in its place, we feel organized and are less likely to lose objects or ideas.

Few leaders have a safe and permanent place for their great ideas. Most say, "I have this great idea. Now, where do I put it?" The Strategic Planning Arrow is the right place to put an idea. Your idea can be very weak, or it can be one of the strongest ideas you've ever had. It's still an idea. Write it down on your Arrow.

When an idea first occurs to me, I often can't determine whether it's a great idea or not. I might later look at my idea list and be embarrassed at the "dumb idea" I wrote down. But occasionally I discover a forgotten but very good idea on my Arrow.

With the Arrow I never have to lose a good idea again. If my idea is a "Christian education idea," I just put it in the Christian education band. If it's a "worship and music idea," I put it in that band. After giving the idea time to mellow and settle down, I can determine whether it is worth pursuing or is worthy only of erasing. Never lose a good idea!

Time Is Money; Ideas Are Also Money

Lawyers tell us, "Time is money!" Time is money, but time is not the only thing that has monetary value. Let me ask you a question: What is a $50,000,000 idea worth the second it's first imagined into being?

If I had $100,000 in the bank, and someone came up to me and said, "Bobb, I have an idea, and I think it's a great idea," I would say, "Wonderful, tell me your idea." And they would say, "Well, I will under one condition. If you use the idea, I want $100,000." I would say, "Well, that sounds pretty steep, but you must have been working on this idea for ever and ever." And they would say, "Nope. Just had it about two minutes ago." Do you know what I'd say? "Fair enough." No matter how new the idea is, if it's the right idea, it could be worth $100,000.

The point is that the right idea is worth a lot of money. Never lose ideas—some of them are very valuable. You may have an idea whose time hasn't come yet. Yet when the time is right, it could be valuable.

There is a story that Henry Ford once hired an efficiency expert to evaluate his company. After a few weeks, the expert made his report. It was highly favorable except for one thing.

"It's that man down the hall," said the expert. "Every time I go by his office he's just sitting there with his feet on his desk. He's wasting your money."

"That man," replied Mr. Ford, "once had an idea that saved us millions of dollars. At the time, I believe his feet were planted right where they are now."

File Backup

There is limited space to write your ideas on the Strategic Planning Arrow. As you flesh out your ideas, create backup files to contain the additional information. You may have several backup files for various ideas on your Arrow. As each file grows and more ideas come together, the original idea may become a goal you want to implement. The Strategic Planning Arrow will not contain all the details of your ideas; it is simply the place to put the essence of the idea or the name of the file.

One of our consulting associates, Terry Fleck, uses three file folders to keep track of his ideas. He has:

1. An "Idea File" of ideas that will probably become priorities or action steps in the near future.

2. A "Thought File" for general thoughts that haven't jelled into good ideas yet. These can be observations that he doesn't want to lose,

but they are not clear ideas.

3. A "Confetti Trap" that catches the ideas that don't fit in the first two categories.

You may have an idea that could raise your visibility in the community. It's only an idea right now, but it could become a priority. You may want to encourage members of your team to run for public office or serve on the school board. You may want to produce a video of the church and its ministries for your members to show to neighbors. You may want to have a booth at the community fair.

You can't act on all these ideas at once, so keep them on your idea list. Pick the best idea, make it a priority, and complete it. Then select the next best idea and execute it. The idea list becomes your reservoir of future priorities.

Caution: Avoid confusing ideas and priorities.

From my perspective, the title of "idea person" is an honor. I love being with "idea people." Yet some people almost spit the phrase with contempt, "Oh, he's just an idea person!" If you are an idea person, like I consider myself to be, you must be careful not to confuse ideas and priorities.

We set ourselves up for great disappointment if we look at every idea as a goal to achieve. We spread our energies so thin that we don't accomplish anything. Part of the beauty of the Strategic Planning Arrow is that it helps us distinguish between ideas and priorities. If you pursue all of your ideas as though they were priorities, you'll overload yourself and burn out.

An Idea Sorter List has been included in Appendix E-2. These questions will help you sift your ideas to determine which ideas should become priorities and which should remain ideas. It will help you, your board, and your staff distinguish between your *good* ideas and your *great* ideas; your someday ideas and your now priorities.

Assignment:

What I'd like you (and/or your team) to do now is set aside this book and have a brainstorming session. Dream up all the ideas you can in each of your objective areas. List every good idea you could someday turn into a priority. Fill up that column. Enjoy!

CHAPTER 9

Arrow Step Six: Roadblocks

Chapter Overview

- Imaginary Roadblocks
- Patterns

As a team leader, one question you need to keep in crystal-clear focus is:

What *three* roadblocks are keeping us from reaching our full potential?

Whether you're leading a company, a university, or a battalion in the military, ask yourself, "What are the three greatest roadblocks keeping us from reaching our full potential as a team?" As a leader, you can't get rid of all your roadblocks at once, so focus on three.

Imaginary Roadblocks

Remember the elephant stake story? The adult elephant learned as a baby that the stake holding its foot wouldn't move. As an adult elephant it doesn't try to lift the stake out of the ground even though it could do so with ease.

Often staff members have roadblocks in their minds that aren't roadblocks in their team leader's mind. Once, I complained to my team leader that I felt I wasn't allowed to carry out a certain course of action that seemed right to me. The team leader saw my obvious irritation and asked, "Bobb, who told you that you can't do what you want to do?"

I said, "Well, I just can't do it."

Again he asked, "Bobb, who told you?"

I said, "No one."

"Then why don't you just do it and stop talking about it?"

It was an "elephant stake," a roadblock in my mind only. Sometimes writing down our assumed roadblocks eliminates a team member's imaginary roadblock.

Patterns

Some roadblocks aren't elephant stakes, but real obstacles to your organization's development. As you identify these true roadblocks in each of your objective areas, you may begin to note a pattern. The roadblock for one objective area may be the same roadblock you find in one or more other objective areas. For example, lack of adequate computer support may hinder you in several objective areas. It is likely that one or two roadblocks are holding you back in every area of your team's development. Your leadership team must focus its energy on dealing with these multiple-area roadblocks.

Years of experience tell me there are probably three common roadblocks facing your leadership. Let me predict that one roadblock will be the *lack of capital*, or money. As a leadership team you need to focus on generating the income that lets you do what you need to do. Another roadblock will be the *lack of available leaders*. Your challenge is training leaders to provide the leadership the team needs to expand in the future. A third may well be facilities. You may find that every one of your departments is crowded and cramped because of a *lack of facilities*.

Assignment:

What are the roadblock patterns in your team? Put this book down once again and consider the question, "What are our top three roadblocks in each objective area?" Then review all of the objective area roadblocks and ask, "What are the top three roadblocks in our whole organization?"

Roadblock #1 _____

Roadblock #2 _____

Roadblock #3 _____

Turn to the "Brainstorming Questions" listed in Appendix E-2 and think of creative ways to eliminate these roadblocks.

CHAPTER 10

Arrow Step Seven: Resources

Chapter Overview

- Keep Your Strengths in Clear Focus
- Patterns
- Speed Modeling
- Use Your Resources to Get Rid of Your Roadblocks

Who do we know who can help us implement our ideas or achieve our priorities? How can we contact them? What seminars, workshops, tape series, and/or consultants would be strong resources to us?

Ask yourself:
What are our *three* greatest resources?

Keep Your Strengths in Clear Focus

One school of leadership development focuses on overcoming weaknesses. This is a negative focus. Do not focus on your weaknesses; instead, focus on maximizing your team's strengths. Place people in their areas of strength, maximizing their strengths 95 percent of the time. Spend 5 percent of the time working on their weaknesses.

Several years ago I attended a three-day retreat with about 25 other organization presidents. Dr. Peter F. Drucker, the famous management expert, was the presenter. One of the points he kept hammering was, "Find out what you are best at and do that." He also made the observation that "The role of the organization is to maximize the strength of the individual and make their weakness irrelevant."

At the time I argued with him (in the privacy of my own mind), *Wait a minute, Peter. I don't agree with you on that one.* I specialized in being a generalist. As a consultant, I had developed expertise in many areas so I could move in many directions and give advice on a wide range of subjects.

But Peter's logic began to burn deeper and deeper into my mind. About three months after the retreat, I spent a fair amount of time concentrating on identifying my greatest strength. I asked some close confidants, "What do you see as my single greatest strength?" I offered to share with each friend what I saw to be her/his primary strength. This exercise brought clarity and has enabled me to make decisions based on my strengths.

Today I pass on to you Dr. Drucker's sage advice. Find what you are best at and do that. The role of your team is ultimately to maximize the strengths of your individual team members and make their weaknesses irrelevant.

Patterns

As you make your list of potential resources available to your team, you will begin to observe patterns in your resources, much as you found patterns in your roadblocks. Look vertically down your resource column and study the patterns—similarities, contrasts, repetitive items—on your resource list.

Speed Modeling

When you identify what your strengths are, build on those strengths. Take what our team calls "Speed Modeling" trips (see Appendix B-6). Find someone else whose strength is the same as your own, or whose team's strengths are the same as your team's, and go visit her/him. As iron sharpens iron, you will learn from each other and strengthen both of your organizations. You can learn more in two days actually watching someone work than you will learn in a week of seminars or in reading five books on the subject.

Find people with strengths that are better developed than yours, that have been in use longer, that have produced more results. If the strength of your administrative department is computer systems, go find people who are even stronger in information technology. As you model people who are stronger than you are, your strengths can be maximized.

Use Your Resources to Get Rid of Your Roadblocks

I define *leadership* as follows:

LEADERSHIP IS KNOWING WHAT TO DO NEXT,
KNOWING WHY THAT IS IMPORTANT,
AND KNOWING HOW TO BRING THE APPROPRIATE
RESOURCES TO BEAR ON THE NEED AT HAND.

You need to eliminate some of your primary roadblocks because they are stopping or substantially slowing progress toward your priorities. Part of the reason the roadblocks and resources columns are parallel to each other is to highlight their interactive nature. As a leader you are constantly bringing your greatest resources to bear on your greatest roadblocks. Identifying both your primary roadblocks and your primary resources is part of the process of problem solving and setting your team free to move forward.

PART THREE

The Doctor Process

Assignment:

Take a few moments now to think, reflect, and pray. Write down possible responses to the question, "What is your single greatest personal strength?" Create a list of 10 or more, and then begin narrowing the list down to your single greatest strength.

_____

_____

_____

_____

_____

_____

Now look at this question from a team-wide perspective. What are your three greatest strengths in each of your objective areas? What are your three greatest strengths as a team?

_____

_____

_____

Welcome back.

- We've developed the point of our Arrow by identifying the needs we care deeply about.

- We've focused our organization by clarifying our purpose and objectives.

- We've put a few "feathers" on our Arrow by listing our milestones, ideas, roadblocks, and resources.

Next we will move on to the shaft of the Strategic Planning Arrow— priorities!

CHAPTER 11

D – Direction

Brain Brander:

Leadership is knowing what to do next,
knowing why that's important,
and knowing how to bring the appropriate
resources to bear on the need at hand.

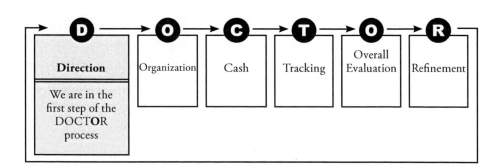

Fog-Cutting Question:

What do we do next?

Chapter Overview

- Priorities (Goals or Problems)
- Frequent Elephant Stakes
- Key Team Transitions in the Directional Phase
- Benefits of Clear Direction
- Priorities: Some Basic Ground Rules
- Good News!
- Establishing Priority Time Frames
    - Short-range Priorities: 0-2 years
    - Mid-range Priorities: 2-5 years
    - Long-range Priorities: 5-20 years
    - Quarterly Priorities: 90 days

Priorities

Bill Owen, a consultant and friend, and I were driving from Los Angeles to Palm Springs, California for a retreat when he casually said, "Bobb, I've come to the conclusion that you can live without priorities…" (My head snapped around so fast that I almost got whiplash. I didn't expect that kind of comment from him.) He continued in his reflective tones, "…if you have no dreams. But, if you have dreams and no priorities, you have only despair." I instantly held my hand up and said, "Don't say another word!" I grabbed my pencil and paper and recorded that moment of brilliance. His thought captured precisely the essence of why defining priorities is so critical.

The Palm Springs desert landscape around us only served to heighten the emotional impact of his statement. How many people do you know who are living lives of despair—lives as desolate as the desert—empty, unfulfilled, dry? They have a dream but never take the time to formulate a few clearly defined priorities—action steps—to move them toward the dream. They live in unnecessary despair.

Over the past 20 years I've talked with many leaders who have grand dreams but no plan to realize them. These individuals drift through life with a fantasy self-promise, "Someday I'm going to accomplish my dream!" Yet if you ask them, "What's step one?" they have no idea. A series of realistic priorities are like a stairway to your dreams.

For many, the phrase "goal setting" triggers a physiological reaction that leaves their stomach in knots. Goal setting equals failure—emotionally, not logically. Our team frequently hears, "Every time I've set goals, I've failed." In the next few pages, I will try to help you pull some elephant stakes that keep you from establishing a clear, step-by-step direction for your dreams.

Frequent Elephant Stakes

ELEPHANT STAKE ONE: "I HATE SETTING GOALS! GOALS EQUAL FAILURE TO ME!"

- Which would you rather do: Reach goals or solve problems?

- Which do you find more energizing: goals or problems?

- Are you a better goal setter or problem solver?

You may be a problem solver rather than a goal setter by nature. If so, you may want to read the book *Stop Setting Goals* for a more detailed understanding of the concept we can only touch on here.

If you are one of the millions of men and women worldwide who prefer solving problems to setting goals, just the word *goals* gives you the feeling that someone has drained all of the energy from your body. I estimate 60 to 90 percent of the world's population prefer problem solving to goal setting. If you are a problem solver, this section is included just for you!

I had been teaching goal setting for over 20 years when one morning I had a "eureka!" experience. I was working with an executive team of about 10 vice presidents at Dave Ray and Associates in Troy, Michigan (the Detroit area). The firm specializes in sophisticated electronic technology, gauges, and guidance systems. The executive team is mostly engineers and sales personnel. I asked each member of the group, "What is your *single greatest strength*? What do you *do* the very best?"

I asked each person to tell the group her/his single greatest strength so the others could know who to call on for that special strength. As they began answering, it was as though each person had been divinely placed to teach me a lesson I had missed for over 20 years.

Half of the people said, in effect,

My strength is reaching goals,

and half said,

My strength is solving problems.

There was no comparing of notes beforehand. It was as though I needed that "live" object lesson to realize that some people naturally see their entire world through the lens of goals, and some through the lens of problems.

Eureka! In a flash of insight, 20 years of frustration caused by trying to teach goal setting to problem solvers dissolved. These problem solvers were not dense, not unable to grasp goal setting. I was dense for not truly understanding problem solvers. This insight opened the door for hundreds of lessons I've learned about goal setters and problem solvers since that life-changing morning.

One such lesson came when I was working with Josh McDowell's team. Josh has spoken live to millions of college students, has written many best-selling books that have sold millions of copies in 75+ languages.

I was teaching his executive team our Leadership Academy. "Stop Setting Goals" was the topic. After the lecture and group discussion, Bob Nickol, a bright 38-year-old vice-president of operations, stopped by to say thanks. He surprised and shocked me with this simple comment: "This has been one of the freest days of my life."

Puzzled, I asked him to help me understand what he meant. He said, "I have hated setting goals ever since I can remember, but I love solving problems. Every time someone asks (or insists) that I set goals, my stomach goes into knots. I get irritable, cranky, kick at the proverbial dog, and generally become miserable to live with. When I am forced to set goals, I find myself wanting to *come to work late and leave early*. I lack natural motivation and energy during the six to twelve hours I do spend grinding it out. If I could define my work as solving problems rather than setting goals, I would want to *come in early and leave late!*"

That morning I was nearly overwhelmed with wondering how many millions of times a day this story is repeated around the world. How much energy is lost with problem solvers who are stuck on goal-setting teams? How many millions or even billions of dollars are wasted daily by de-motivated problem solvers who are forced to set goals?

Problem solvers frequently feel like second-class citizens in the shadow of goal setters and the goal-setting orientation that has become standard in corporate culture and even in many national cultures. Problem solvers are not second-class citizens. They are the defensive unit of the team that complements the offensive unit (goal setters). Both goal setters and problem solvers are absolutely indispensable whenever you want to win in the games of life!

> ### Important Note to Goal Setters:
>
> Keep setting goals to focus your future, but encourage the problem solvers on your team to focus their future by defining the problems they will solve instead of the goals they will reach!

Do you feel more naturally energized by goals and drained by problems? Or do you feel more naturally energized by problems and drained by goals? If you can identify yourself as a goal setter or a problem solver and then work within your preferences, you and any team you lead will experience:

- Maximized "natural energy"
- Reduced conflict, tension, and anxiety
- Increased productivity
- Increased team spirit, morale, and respect
- Improved communication
- Increased confidence

The implications of letting goal setters set goals and problem solvers solve problems are enormous. Consider the implications of the above benefits for:

- A professional sports team
- A major computer company's executive team
- The office team of a local high school principal
- The staff of a governor, senator, or congressman
- Any team on which you choose to play—your team!

You may ask the legitimate question, "What is the difference between goals and problems if both are measurable?"

	Goals	Problems
Definition	Taking the existing system and adding something new to it.	Taking the existing system and fixing some problem within it.
Example	Taking your existing building and adding a new wing, or buying an additional piece of property.	Taking your existing facility and fixing the air conditioning, repaving the parking lot, or repainting the building.
Results	Clear focus. High motivation for the goal setter. Measurable major accomplishment when finished.	Clear focus. High motivation for the problem solver. Measurable major accomplishment when finished.

ELEPHANT STAKE TWO: "I'M NOT GOOD AT GOAL SETTING."

Focus on realistic, measurable goals *or* problems. What we are going to do in this section is to encourage you to set realistic goals or define realistic problems you will solve. We're not talking about pie-in-the-sky priorities, trying to impress people with the goals you set or problems you define. Our aim is simply to determine realistic, measurable goals or problems.

ELEPHANT STAKE THREE: "WHO REALLY KNOWS WHAT WILL HAPPEN TWO TO 20 YEARS FROM NOW? WHY PLAN?"

The primary function of planning is to provide a clear, single direction that helps everyone in the organization focus in the same direction. You may not reach all your long-range priorities, but aiming at them will help you head in the right direction.

The chances of reaching all your 20-year priorities are probably 10 percent. It would be unreasonable to expect to reach 100 percent of your priorities. Many variables in your planning will change over 20 years. Some resources will disappear; some will greatly increase. New opportunities and needs will arise. Still, projecting a long-range plan based on realistic variables today will free you to initiate rather than react.

Key Team Transitions in the Directional Phase

A group will go through several pivotal transitions when it starts creating a Strategic Plan. Three of the most significant are:

PAST/PRESENT —> FUTURE

You will move from relying on, living in, or being concerned about the past, or feeling stuck in the present, to focusing on the future—just by starting the planning process. You will move from resting on your laurels to stretching toward the future, and from the nostalgia and melancholy of past reflections to the exciting possibilities of the future!

WHAT IS —> WHAT IF

You will move from a resigned acceptance of your current circumstances—"This is the way we have always done it," "This is only reality," "I don't know what else we can do about it"—to possibilities, plans, and dreams! Team members begin to get excited as they see what could be—what our generation of leadership could contribute to history.

REACTIVE —> PROACTIVE

You will move from drowning in the urgent to focusing on the important. No longer only responding to the complaints and demands of a few "squeaking people," you will be able to initiate improvements for the whole team. You will move from feeling overwhelmed and "under the pile" to being "on top of the pile" with a smile!

Benefits of Clear Direction

Your organization will experience numerous benefits from establishing a clear direction.

BENEFIT ONE: INCREASED CONFIDENCE IN MOVING FROM A PAST TO FUTURE FOCUS

Determining a directional statement for your organization is one of the most critical, frightening, and satisfying moves in all of leadership. It is a process of moving from response to initiation, from fire fighting to clear direction. It is one of the most fundamental changes that leadership brings. It is moving from "just getting by" to "winning big"!

BENEFIT TWO: CLEARER CONTEXT FOR WISE DECISION MAKING

As a team, once you decide whether you are going to keep growing or intentionally slow the growth curve, you can make wiser decisions concerning building programs, hiring staff, and so on. You will have a clear context for decision making.

BENEFIT THREE: INCREASED MOTIVATION WHEN YOU SEE YOU ARE COMING OUT OF A "FOG"

When you have a clear direction you are free to dream, innovate, and make decisions. It gets exciting! You may be working in an organization that lacks clarity, vision, and direction. As a leader you may be saying, "This place is a mess! No one knows what they are doing. It feels like we are drowning in a sea of confusion." I say, "Great! Create an island of clarity in the sea of confusion."

Do what you are supposed to do regardless of what your board, your staff, or your peers do. Begin to create an island on which you are clear about what you are doing. It doesn't matter if every other leader in your district, region, or nation is not clear about their direction. You become clear about *your* direction.

Effective leadership is one of the valuable by-products of clear direction. I met a man who worked his way through seminary making three thousand dollars a day as a consultant to NASA—not your average person. I asked him, "If you could know only one thing about an organization and predict its success or failure, what would you want to know?" He said, "I'd ask to meet their leader and their leadership team. Then I would ask to see their goals/priorities."

When you formulate a clear plan with which you, your board, and your staff agree 100 percent, you are going to unlock a deep excitement about the future!

Priorities: Some Basic Ground Rules

PRIORITIES SHOULD BE MEASURABLE... OR THEY ARE ONLY GOOD INTENTIONS

There is something comforting—and motivating—when we get to the end of a year and are able to say, "I did what I planned to do." Reaching one's priorities doesn't imply that you're perfect, it just says you achieved a certain measurable priority.

You set yourself up for failure if you don't make your priorities measurable. People often unintentionally design failure into their priorities by writing them as good intentions. "I want to do better next year." "We want to do the best we can." "I want to share my faith more." "I want to sell as much as I can." These are good intentions, but they are by definition not priorities because they are not measurable!

Without measurable priorities, you cannot accurately assess your progress. There is also no accountability. I can easily excuse the lack of progress with vague explanations of extraordinary complications or encumbrances. "I did the best I could given the circumstances."

You may be saying to yourself, "Well, you can't measure everything, Bobb." Absolutely right! I agree 100 percent! But there are many things we can measure, even in the spiritual area, that let us know if we have made progress. The most important things in life are *not* measurable, but we can try to measure the part of the process we control. For example, we don't measure God's response to our prayers, but we can measure how many days we pray consistently. We control how much we pray; God controls the answers.

Priorities Should Be Written in Pencil, Not in Stone

Another thing Bill Owen taught me was: *Priorities should be in sand, and our purpose in concrete; not the other way around.* Some people put their priorities in concrete and their purpose in sand. They are always shifting their direction, but they hang onto those priorities.

Times change. Circumstances change. Needs change. Life is constantly changing! You see a need that highly motivates you, and you determine to do something about it. You set some priorities to achieve a solution to the need. Over time, the priority may need revising because the resources or opportunities may change for the better or the worse. No problem—priorities are written in pencil. Flip your pencil over and erase the priority. Rewrite it to keep you moving toward meeting the need you want to meet.

There is an ancient Chinese proverb that says,

A man who would know the future three days in advance, his family would be wealthy for generations.

No one knows what is going to happen tomorrow. The economy may fall, the economy may surge. But, based on today's realities, establish the priorities that are realistic for your leadership team.

Priorities belong in pencil or in easy-to-delete word processing. Don't be frightened by a clearly written, measurable priority (goal or problem). When you write a priority and type it out so other people can read it, it is not in concrete. It is not something that you have to do. You don't have to feel like a dismal failure if you don't achieve it. See priorities as targets you are aiming at today.

PRIORITIES SHOULD BE VISIBLE OR IT IS EASY TO SLIP OFF TRACK

Keep your priorities visible. Many people define priorities, then misplace them in a drawer. You don't have to display your priorities on your office wall for the world to see, but you do need to keep your list where you will be reminded frequently of these high priorities for the future.

PRIORITIES SHOULD BE KEPT WITH YOU FOR FREQUENT REVIEW

I have my 90-day priorities with me 99 percent of the time. If you ever meet me anywhere, at any time, feel free to ask me, "Let me see your 90-day priorities." Chances are I'll have them with me, and they'll be up-to-date. Visible 90-day priorities keep me focused on a day-to-day basis. When my to-do list gets close to getting done, I always go back to my 90-day priorities and say, "All right, what can I to keep chipping away at these?

WHY PEOPLE SET UNREALISTIC PRIORITIES

One of the common reasons people set unrealistic priorities is that *they define priorities when they are emotionally high* (i.e., at the end of an exciting sales meeting). They feel like they can conquer the world, so to speak. They define lofty, exciting priorities, but they don't have any idea how they will ever achieve them. Beware of defining your priorities when you are on an emotional high. If you sense you're emotionally "in the clouds," go ahead and dream, but avoid setting priorities. Wait until you come down a bit.

Another reason people set unrealistic priorities is that *they have no experience, no track record in a particular area*. When I lecture on the DOCTOR process, I have a little warning for the class.

---

*Until you have milked a cow,
don't brag about how many gallons
you can get the first hour.*

Have you ever milked a cow? Let me tell you my personal experience with this noble task. When I was about nine years old, I stayed overnight at my friend Larry Gates' house. Larry's family had a couple of cows. I thought to myself, *I can milk these cows; farmers have done it for centuries; my friend Larry does it every morning before breakfast. How hard can it be?* About 4:00 in the morning, Larry and I went to the barn. I watched Larry. He was doing just fine. You know, squirt, squirt, squirt. It looked easy. So I sat down on this little three-legged stool near the udder. I started to squeeze, and just then Blue Roam put her manure-encrusted tail right across my face. Finally I got the first squirt—it went straight to the floor! After about half an hour I successfully landed about three squirts in the otherwise empty pail. And my forearms ached for days.

Be careful when setting priorities in an area of activity where you don't have some kind of track record. Too often we go into a new situation and set priorities that are very unrealistic. If you don't have a track record, set low priorities.

A third reason many people set unrealistically high priorities is *to impress the manager*. Team members like to impress or please team leaders. This is natural and positive. A leader may define higher priorities than he/she can reach because he/she wants to impress or please the board. But this approach is often a short-lived victory when six months later the unrealistically high priority isn't reached. He/she now feels like a failure in the board's eyes.

A fourth reason we set unrealistically high priorities is *to motivate ourselves*—"Reach for the stars, and you'll at least hit the moon." We are trying to motivate ourselves into doing what we think we should be able to do. My experience confirms, if you try to reach the stars without a rocket, you will only end up in fatigue trying to jump to the moon. You may get two or three feet off the ground several times, but you won't reach the moon. Far better to be realistic. Define priorities that will encourage you and your team, not discourage you.

Good News!

You don't have to be perfect to make a big difference. You don't have to achieve every priority to make a significant difference in a year.

Your organization has hired you by the year, not by the day. Every day doesn't have to be perfect—and it won't be!

You don't have to be "up" all the time. Some people, particularly "positive mental attitude" people, are shocked when I say that if you have only 250 good days a year—days when you are feeling wonderful, on top of it, ready to conquer the world—you are in great shape. You will have days when you are a little discouraged, don't feel well, want to stay home and have your spouse pat you affectionately and say, "You're a good person." There's nothing wrong with it! We all go through days like this. Why not admit it? It's okay not to be the perfect super-leader. Allow your board members a few discouraged days, your staff a few discouraged days, your spouse a few discouraged days. This is reality, even for world-class leaders.

It's okay not to reach all your priorities (goals or problems). Several years ago I set 10 goals for myself (I enjoy setting goals!). At the end of the year, I had achieved five of the goals. Three I hadn't reached yet, but I was gaining on them; I just missed on the timing. For two of the priorities, the situation changed so much I abandoned them. I did pick up a couple more priorities along the way. It turned out to be a very good year. The point is that I rarely reach all of the goals I set at the beginning of a year.

Establishing Priority Time Frames

Theoretically all planning begins at the end. Unless you know where you want to end up it is impossible for you to know the wisest step to take today. Some members of your team find it easier to start with a 20-year look at the organization. This 20-year look at your organization is often very inspiring. It sets up an excitement that energizes your shorter-range planning.

Some groups actually find it easier to look 50 years ahead. Will future members say, "We are thankful the board did this or that 50 years ago" or "If only the board 50 years ago had bought this piece of property"?

Whether your team finds it easier to look 20 years or 50 years into the future or prefers to start where you are and move step-by-step into the future is up to you.

Either way, let me suggest that you skip the 90-day priorities in your process, even though it's next on the Arrow. If your team finds it hard to get started on a 20-to-50 year view of your church, our team has found that it may be easier to start with your two-year priorities, then the five-year, and then the 20-year, and then return to the 90-day priorities. You can start anywhere on the Strategic Planning Arrow that you find most comfortable, but, for now, let's start by looking at two-year priorities.

Short-Range Priorities: Zero to Two Years

In the next zero to two years, what are our three most important, measurable, realistic targets of accomplishment?

AGREE ON DEFINITIONS

As we discussed a few pages ago, purpose, objectives, and priorities mean something different depending on where a person works. Success, happiness, and leadership also have different meanings to different people. We are about to look at three more phrases for which there is no standard meaning when it comes to planning: short-range, mid-range, and long-range priorities.

To some leaders, a short-range priority is two years away. To others it's a year, 90 days, or even five years. Participants in a "futurist's think-tank" might say, "Our short-range priorities are 100 years, our mid-range priorities are 200, and our long-range priorities are 300 years into the future." On a six-month project, you might say, "Our short-range priorities are one month, our mid-range priorities are one to three months, and our long-range priorities are three to six months."

Each enterprise, corporation, organization, or church has to define the length of time assumed in short-, mid-, and long-range priorities.

For the purpose of your planning, your team can decide for itself just how long a short-range goal will be. In nonprofit organizations, and churches in particular, our consulting team has found that most boards feel comfortable with a one-to-two-year time frame for short-range priorities.

Caution: A nonprofit organization or a church will typically accomplish in *two years* what it hopes to accomplish in *one year*. Most priorities in a nonprofit organization are set assuming that staff will be trained and in place, that the budget will be approved, and that the income will be adequate. Typically, however, the income doesn't come in, or you can't find the key staff member you had planned to hire, or any number of other unforeseen events interfere with your plan. A year passes and you find yourself just getting started with what you had planned to do the first part of the year. Accomplishing that priority takes another year. As a leadership team, don't be frustrated with your staff and your unpaid team member team if things take longer than planned.

What do You Need to do Today to Reach Your Dreams?

However you define short-range priorities, the question remains: In the next zero to two years, what are our top *three* measurable, realistic targets of accomplishment? A short-range priority has a 50 to 70 percent chance of happening as written initially. Factor this percentage range into your plans. Things change! People change, money changes, economies change, communities change. And as the facts change, so will your plans.

A short-range priority is part of the foundation of your 20-year dreams. Project yourselves as a leadership team 20 years into the future. Imagine yourselves sitting around with a little more gray hair, or a little less hair, looking back on this year and saying, "You know, what really set us up for today were those three things we did 20 years ago. Remember when we bought that property we didn't think we were going to need? Remember when we built our first unit? Remember when we did this, or that? Those three things formed the base of what we have become."

When you look ahead 20 years, it seems like a very long time. But when you look back 20 years, it seems like a very short time. As you imagine looking back 20 years from now, what will you wish you had done today to get your organization ready for that time period? What will the organization of the future see that you did right today?

SET YOUR SHORT-RANGE PLAN OF ACTION

Short-range priorities have a maximum of three priorities per objective area. Some objective areas may only have one priority while others may not have any, because you do not plan to target that area in the next two years. When you are completing draft one of your Strategic Planning Arrow, ask, "Of all the things we could do in Christian education, of all the things we could do in administration, and so forth, what are the top three things we want to do in the next two years?" This is the simple, clear question we are seeking to answer.

Some examples of short-range priorities may be helpful (priorities are always started with action verbs):

- Establish a second Sunday morning worship service by September next year.

- Hire a full-time associate pastor by July next year.

- Conduct a couples retreat this fall.

- Initiate a capital campaign for our new building within two years.

- Host a "Leadership Training" seminar for all area churches in April, two years from now.

Personal priorities might include:

- Lose fifteen pounds.

- Read the Bible through once each year for the next two years.

- Spend one day a month in a personal prayer and planning retreat.

- Read one book a week.

Write your priorities in measurable terms on your Arrow so in two years you will know whether you accomplished them or not. See your priorities as written in pencil. If you get sick or unexpected responsibilities come your way, you won't be too frustrated when some priorities need to be neglected. Keep your priorities visible as daily reminders. Carry your Arrow with your calendar or in your attaché case. Review your priorities often, remembering to erase completed priorities and add them to your milestone list.

Assignment:

It's time to set this book aside and think about your answers to the question, "In the next two years, what three things do we want to accomplish in each of our objective areas that are measurable, in pencil, and realistic?"

Mid-Range Priorities: Two to Five Years

In the next two to five years, what are our three most important, measurable, realistic targets of accomplishment?

KEEP YOUR PRIORITIES IN PENCIL

Sixty to 80 percent of leadership is dealing with plans in some stage of change. Little remains static in life. We set out to do something, but it seldom turns out exactly the way we planned. We evolve it into the next phase, and then the next phase. Your priorities will develop clarity with each revision. Just because a priority is written on paper in a two-to-five-year range doesn't mean you can't adjust it based on new realities.

Remember, too, on your Strategic Planning Arrow priorities are always interchangeable with ideas.

MAINTAIN FLEXIBILITY

What if three months from now you see that what you thought was a two-to-five-year priority should be made a 90-day priority? Another priority you thought was going to be a 90-day goal could be erased and moved to the two-to-five-year range. What do you do?

Your priorities are in pencil, remember? Simply change them and alert the board of your change. If it's acceptable to them, consider it done!

Work Within a Closed System

The Strategic Planning Arrow is a very flexible planning process and at the same time, it is a closed system. Once an idea is on your Strategic Planning Arrow, it can become a 20-year priority, then a two-to-five-year priority, a two-year priority, a 90-day priority, and finally a milestone. Your ideas remain on your Strategic Planning Arrow from their inception until they become milestones. Every great idea you have can become a milestone as it works its way through the system at the appropriate time. That may be seventeen years from now, but you haven't lost a great idea.

Assignment:

It's time to try to answer the question, "What are our top three priorities per objective area for the next two to five years?"

Welcome back. Now we are going to look at long-range priorities.

Long-Range Priorities:
Five to Twenty Years

What three measurable, realistic priorities are you dreaming of accomplishing five to 20 years from now?

Agree on an Approximate Size

Long-range priorities have only a 10 to 30 percent chance of happening as originally written. Why, then, would we even begin to try to project a 20-year priority? Practically speaking, it allows a group to agree on an "approximate size," a general direction for the future.

As we discussed at the beginning of this book, your leadership team will hold wildly varying assumptions about your organization's future. Three board members are thinking, "In 20 years the church membership will probably be approximately 400 people." Another four people are thinking, "It will probably be 4000 people." And two people over here are thinking, "I think by then our church could be influencing approximately four million people in a worldwide tape, television, radio, and literature distribution ministry."

Without an agreement on "approximate size," your organization will have conflict and tension all the time. Based on their differing assumptions about the long-range future, one's going to say, "I think we should add a part-time assistant this year." The other one will say, "I think we need to add five full-time assistants."

If you can agree on an approximate size you can move ahead with clarity and confidence. Projecting 20 years down the road with "broad brush strokes" will help. If you can agree on such basic questions as, "Do we want a school or not?" or "What potential growth could we experience?" you will have a much clearer context for day-to-day decision making.

Avoid Comparisons with Your Past or Your Peers.

Compare yourself with your own potential and the needs you see in order to gain a realistic dream for the future. As you are dreaming, don't say, "Well, compared to the xyz, we're doing great now," or "We have come a very long way in the past five years!" True! But, don't look at life that way. Look at your situation and ask, "What is the size of the need within a few miles of our church, or in our parish area, or whatever is appropriate for our church? What are the needs? How do we want to affect these needs?"

People have asked me many times, "Bobb, how big should our group become?" I say, "I don't know how big your business, church, or organization should be. How large is the need?" Look at the needs you see and the potential for your services. Don't look at your past. If you look at your past, you probably will get proud of where you already are. Don't look at your peers, because you are probably already ahead of them. Look at the needs and the opportunities, and then decide just how big your dreams should be!

Put this book down and spend about 10 minutes imagining what life would be like if we could accomplish all our priorities. Then consider what your top three long-range priorities for each objective will be.

Quarterly Priorities: Ninety-Days

In the next 90 days, what are our three most important measurable, realistic targets of accomplishment?

Most leaders set quarterly priorities in their normal planning process. I do this by taking my two-year priorities from the Arrow and breaking them down into a "carryable" version of 90-day priorities, which I write on the Strategic Planning Arrow.

Assignment:

Consider what your top three quarterly priorities for each objective will be.

Congratulations on defining your future priorities! Now, let's talk about your organizational structures and team development to turn your priorities into milestones in the future.

It's time for a brain break!

*God's timing is perfect—
even when it differs from my plans!*

CHAPTER 12

O – Organization

Brain Brander:

*The key to building a great team
is getting round pegs in round holes
of approximately the same size.*

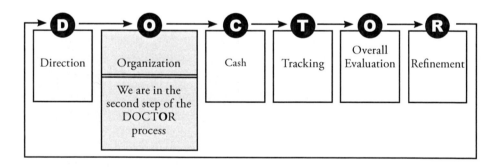

Fog-Cutting Questions:

Who is responsible for what?

Who is responsible for whom?

Do we have the right people in the right places?

Chapter Overview

- Key Team Transitions in the Organizational Phase
- Frequent Elephant Stakes
- Benefits of Clear Organization
- Historic Models of Organization
- "Rules of Thumb" in Designing an Organizational Chart
- Key Organizational Chart Terms
- An Organizational Chart Is a Framework for...
- Tool Two: Organizational Chart
- Tool Three: Position Focus Sheet

Warning: Several years ago I agreed to create an audio cassette tape series called "Strategic Planning Your Church." Before I agreed to do this, I struggled with the question, "Is it realistic for a person to work through the Strategic Planning process without one of our consultants available to provide objectivity?" I was not concerned about the direction section, the cash, or any other component, but the organization section.

One of the main benefits of a consultant is objectivity. It is very difficult to remain objective when building a team. Families get involved—husbands, wives, and children. Loyalties build up over the years. You have people in positions who should have been relieved a long time ago but are loved by the team. Everyone knows that they are not doing their position, but no one knows how to relieve them of that responsibility. Team chemistry is a personal, subjective feeling. Without outside perspective and counsel, it is almost impossible to gain objectivity on your own team.

Do draft one of your organizational chart and team placement. Then if you have any division, pressure, or frustration while starting to build your team, invite one of our consultants to come in for a day to guide you through the organizational step. If you don't get the right team together, it's very difficult to carry out the directional plans!

Key Team Transitions in the Organizational Phase

There are several key team transitions while building a strong team. When each person feels like a round peg in a round hole of just the right size you will see the following changes:

CAN DO —> WANT TO

When people find just where they fit, they are able to move from "what they can do if pressed hard enough" to "what they want to do to make a difference!" Motivationally, these are very different. Getting people into positions where they really fit increases their natural energy level substantially.

MORALE PROBLEMS —> MOTIVATED TEAM

When people on a team find just where they fit and have clear priorities, there is a significant change in the entire team's attitude. They move from droopy, draggy, and down to motivated, energized, and up!

SUPERSTARS —> "SUPER BOWL" TEAM

When each person knows her/his own position, feels like part of the dream, and "pulls her/his own weight," a group of individuals becomes a team. Superstars become players on a "super bowl" team. This is major progress!

Frequent Elephant Stakes

ELEPHANT STAKE ONE: "I'VE JUST NEVER BEEN GOOD AT GETTING THE 'RIGHT PEOPLE IN THE RIGHT PLACE.'"

We're going to help you know how to "get round pegs in round holes" in this section. In the next few minutes you are going to learn how to define a position and get the right person for that position.

ELEPHANT STAKE TWO: "I DON'T NEED A LARGE (SIXTY-BOX) ORGANIZATIONAL CHART. I ONLY HAVE A FEW FULL-TIME STAFF PEOPLE."

Your organizational chart needs to include your plans for the future. When you start an organization by yourself, your name is in every one of the boxes. As full-time or nonpaid staff *(volunteers)* come along who can assume a responsibility, you can put their name in the box. Having a complete organizational chart helps new people see exactly where they fit.

ELEPHANT STAKE THREE: "UNPAID TEAM MEMBERS ARE SO APATHETIC—WHY BOTHER?"

Many years ago I actually bought into the "unpaid team member apathy" myth. Today, I have become absolutely convinced that unpaid team member apathy is not a cause but a symptom. The cause of unpaid team member apathy is the inability of leadership to organize work and understand how to plug "round pegs into round holes of the right size." When they are given the right task, they are excited, self-motivated, and self-directed. When they are asked to be a round peg in a square hole, they have an understandably apathetic response.

Imagine 50 highly qualified staff (paid or unpaid) come to you today and say, "We will do anything you ask for as long as you want us to. We will remain 100 percent positive, enthusiastic, and focused. Just tell us specifically what to do in a way that maximizes each of our abilities." Would you be confident in your ability to put them in the right slots?

There are two ways to use an organizational chart. One way creates apathy; the other generates excitement. Suppose an unpaid team member comes to you and expresses an interest in becoming involved. You look at your chart, see the most pressing vacancy, and fill that slot with your unpaid team member. If you mismatch the task and the person's talents, apathy will result. But if you look at the organizational chart and find the position most closely aligned to her/his interests and abilities, you will have an eager, capable team member.

I have found healthy, dynamic, growing organizations have one thing in common. They have found a way to free unpaid team members to work in their areas of strength, thus doing away with apathy. The result is a highly motivated team of paid and unpaid members.

Benefits of Clear Organization

BENEFIT ONE: INCREASES TEAM SPIRIT—UNITY

An organizational chart makes clear to everyone who is responsible for what and who is responsible for whom. It is like a playing roster for a sports team. Everyone knows what her/his position is and what the relationship of the position is to all of the other positions on the team. It is this knowledge that lets people play together in precision, harmony, and unity.

The organizational chart also strengthens your team's diversity. If everyone is trying to do the same thing, you'll have competitiveness, not unity. Again, learn from a football or baseball team. Different positions, or tasks, are assigned to each player. When players fulfill their roles, the team can function as a winning unit. Unity is the result of diversity, not uniformity.

BENEFIT TWO: REDUCES BURNOUT

Burnout has become one of the heartbreaking realities of our time. Far too many leaders are on the verge of burnout. Several close friends of mine have gone through that devastating process. An organizational chart is a key tool to reduce burnout.

Every leader I've known who burned out didn't know how to build a team. They tried to do everything. When I ask them to draw an organizational chart of their organization, the problem becomes clear. The person's "span of control" was much too large.

An organizational chart visually reveals the number of people for whom an individual is responsible. "Span of control" is a business principle that explains much of the burned out leader's experience. How many people report directly to you? How many people can't function without your input and decision? This is your span of control.

During organizational transition, give attention to the span of control expected of each individual on the leadership team. This is especially true in an organization that is experiencing rapid growth. Here are several rules of thumb as to how many people you should ask a leader to manage:

7:1: Mature Executive/Leadership Team

The mature executive can typically manage a leadership team of seven people. If you want highly productive leaders on your team, you need people who are living healthy, balanced lives—people who are growing professionally and personally. It will take an investment of your time to help them grow and function together as a team. You can't invest that kind of time with 20 people, but you can with seven. If you have a whole roomful of assembly workers doing exactly the same thing, you can possibly manage them on a day-to-day basis at 20:1, 30:1, or maybe even more. When it comes to developing team member's leadership skills, most leaders can manage only seven people.

5:1: New Staff

If you have an inexperienced team, they will demand more of you than would a seasoned team. Therefore, with a new staff, your span of control or supervision should be less—let's say a 5:1 ratio.

In a "start up" situation, the tendency is for the chief executive to have responsibility for more people than is recommended. "Well, I don't have the right leadership, therefore I have 10 people reporting to me, and they are all new." It doesn't take long to burn out in a growing organization where everyone reports to one person.

3:1: Unpaid Manager

Even though a person may be a school superintendent in day-to-day work and supervise several hundred teachers, when that person serves your team as an unpaid team leader, don't ask her/him to manage another seven people. A unpaid team member with five or 10 hours a week to give can't manage many people. The maximum number as a rule of thumb would be a 3:1 ratio. Ask an experienced but unpaid leader to manage three people, not seven.

Benefit Three: Reduces Frustration, Pressure, and Tension by Creating the Same Assumptions of Roles and Responsibilities

According to Dr. Jerry Ballard, "All miscommunication is the result of differing assumptions." Miscommunication results in frustration, pressure, and tension. When an organizational chart spells out who is responsible for what and who is responsible for whom, it drastically reduces the number of differing assumptions, thus drastically reducing the amount of miscommunications, thus drastically reducing the amount of frustration, pressure, and tension felt within your team.

Historic Models of Organization

If you are introducing organizational charts to a leadership team, consider using these three Scripture passages for biblical models of organization.

Division of Labor Reduces Burnout: Ex. 18:13–26

Moses was working day and night. His father-in-law Jethro approached Moses and essentially warned him, "If you don't watch out Moses, you are going to burn out. You are working from early morning to late at night. You are seeing all the people who have any kind of problem. What you need to do is to divide up the people. Have a few people who answer to you oversee others, who oversee others, until every 10 people have an overseer. Develop statutes (policies or procedures) by which these leaders will govern. If you divide your labor this way you will avoid burnout or an early heart attack, and will be a better husband for my daughter and a better father for my grandchildren."

You get the point, right? If you read on through Exodus, those policies and procedures for making decisions are clearly defined. Moses was then free to deal with the issues no one else could handle.

No Task Too Large: Nehemiah's Model

Rebuilding the walls of Jerusalem was a huge task, somewhat equivalent to building the Great Wall of China. Nehemiah identified all the tasks necessary to rebuild the wall and then divided the labor force to address all the tasks (see Nehemiah 2–6).

Attitude of Organization: 1 Corinthians 12:14–27

This classic text of the apostle Paul describes the essential parts of a human body as a model of organization. Every part is important and necessary. "The eye cannot say to the hand, 'I don't need you!'" (v. 21, NIV).

"Rules of Thumb" in Designing an Organizational Chart

Following a few "rules of thumb" will help you avoid numerous pitfalls as you design your organizational chart.

One Person per Box. No co-captains! Rarely does a co-captain—an arrangement that shares responsibility—work well. You don't want two people responsible for any single function. They will compete, or one will lead and the other follow.

One Box per Person/One Person to Please. When one person reports to two people, you create a situation of high stress for that first individual. It is common for one assistant to be to asked to report to two executives. This will work fine if you define very clearly when the assistant reports primarily to executive number one (i.e., Monday, Wednesday, Friday, or mornings) and when the assistant reports primarily to executive number two. If one person reports to two executives at the same time, it will create a great deal of pressure when both executives want something on the same time schedule.

Paid vs. Unpaid. Often a team leader will ask, "Do I treat an unpaid or a part-time staff person differently than a full-time, paid staff member?" The main difference between a paid staff member and an unpaid team member is the amount of time they have to give. A paid person is offering you 40 to 60 hours a week in exchange for a livelihood. The unpaid team member is offering you less than 20 hours a week. Treat both basically the same. Treat unpaid team members as though they were paid staff. They are just available fewer hours per week.

Review from Top Down

Whenever you are reviewing an organization, start from the top. Don't ever forget:

Every organizational unit is a direct reflection of the leadership it has been given, for good or for bad.

This is true whether it's a department, a division, a church, a denomination, or a major manufacturing facility. Any organization is a direct reflection of its leadership. So whenever you're reviewing, start with the board, then the senior executive, and on down.

ALPHABETIZE DEPARTMENTS

For what am I responsible? For what are you responsible? These are reasonable questions, responsible questions. When we see our relationship with another person through competitive eyes, we create an unhealthy team relationship.

One way to help avoid this competitive one-upmanship on a team is to alphabetize the departments. People tend to view "higher" positions on an organizational chart as more important. When you alphabetize departments, it helps defuse competitive reactions.

Key Organizational Chart Terms

Unlike other planning terms (purpose, objective, priorities), the words and concepts used in creating an organizational chart are fairly standard. Most business environments—educational, military, corporate—will use these terms to mean much the same thing.

PRIMARY RESPONSIBILITY

An organizational chart is primarily a "picture" of relationships based on responsibility. It is a chart of "primary responsibility." The Christian education director may sing in the choir, and the choir director may teach a Sunday school class. Cooperation and participation between boxes other than the one you direct is an assumed part of life. It doesn't show up on the chart, but it is implied.

At the end of the year, you are not going to ask the music director why s/he didn't get better results in Christian education, or the Christian education director why the choir didn't sound better. Your questions will be directed to the one *primarily responsible* for that specific area. It is her/his name that shows up on the organizational chart indicating the area for which s/he is responsible.

An organizational chart is also frequently called an "Org Chart" in day-to-day conversation, but it should never be referred to as a flow chart. A "flow chart" is the same as a "process chart," not an organizational chart.

LINE POSITION

A "line" position on an organizational chart indicates that this person has primary responsibility for setting priorities in this department. A Christian education director may be responsible to define her/his own priorities in the area of Christian education in agreement with the senior pastor and approved by the board. A "line" position has responsibility to define and reach priorities. For a "line" position, the connecting line in an organizational chart comes into the top of the box.

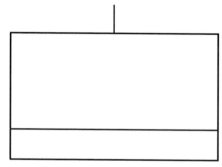

STAFF POSITION

The primary difference between a "line" position and a "staff" position is responsibility for setting priorities. The "line" position sets her/his own priorities; a "staff" position's priorities are set by someone else. A typical "staff" position would be a secretary, administrative assistant, executive assistant, personal assistant, or research assistant. Their primary focus or responsibility is to be supportive of the team leader's priorities. The connecting line for the "staff" position comes into the side of the box.

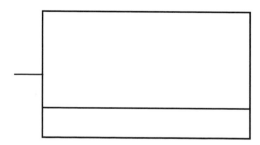

Staff/Line Position

A "staff/line" position is primarily supportive but is responsible for its own priorities. An example would be an administrative services department. The administrative services department has its own priorities. The administrative services director needs to establish very clear measurable priorities. But, these priorities are all in support of the rest of the team. Compare this to an administrative assistant who is hired to support a manager but is expected to establish no priorities of her/his own.

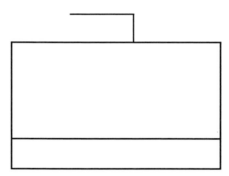

Projected Planning (On the Drawing Board)

Your organizational chart will primarily reflect what presently exists in your organization. You can picture future planning and positions you want to create by using a box of dotted lines.

DOTTED LINES BETWEEN BOXES

Unless there is some particular need for it, you *do not* have to show dotted lines between all the positions on the organizational chart. It's assumed that the department directors will have frequent communications, friendly relations, and no authority over one another. But let's say, for example, you had a consulting firm, the accountant, or the attorney come in to advise the senior executive. An accounting, legal, or planning position may exist on your chart, and a dotted line would connect the position to the senior executive. A dotted line indicates significant communication but no authority.

"ACTING" POSITION

If you are going to assign someone to a position on a temporary basis, you might want to use the term "acting director" or "acting coordinator." Teach your whole team that the "acting" term means, "We are going to try it for a while. The person assigned may not like the position; the person assigned may not do well in the position; or the person assigned and the team leader may both agree it is best to go back to the way it was." An individual is allowed to return to her/his former position with no implied failure or sense of embarrassment.

An Organizational Chart
Is a Framework for:

HIRING, FIRING, OR REASSIGNING

The organizational chart is a critical planning tool. It is the basis or context for hiring, firing, and reassigning people in the organization. "Of all the positions on our organizational chart, which one do we need to hire next?" Charts help you visualize the next steps in hiring.

"If we release this person, how will it impact the organization?" Organizational charts help you see the impact of releasing staff. Review all the positions on your organizational chart and evaluate the personnel. Color code the staff. Green means they are the right person in the right place, long term. Yellow means they may need to change. Red means they should have been gone days, weeks, even years ago. This color-coded chart is obviously for your eyes only. It should not be shown to your staff or to the public.

As you evaluate your staff and their positions, you may want to consider reassigning people to more appropriate positions. Your chart will help you visualize the changes before you start reassigning people or reorganizing the office. Imagine your staff changes on paper first. It's far easier on you and your staff to reorganize the names on paper in the privacy of your own office than it is to start moving offices and desks, and then change your mind.

SETTING PRIORITIES

Once you know what you're responsible for, you can say, "All right, now I can begin setting the priorities in this area." For example, if you are responsible for accounting and bookkeeping you can ask yourself, "What three realistic measurable things do we need to accomplish in the accounting and bookkeeping area?" You do not have to worry about any other person's area of responsibility.

ORGANIZATIONAL COMMUNICATIONS FLOW (REPORTING)

Who is responsible to tell what to whom? Your chart communicates the organizational communications flow, or which lead positions will be responsible to keep their staff appropriately informed. When announcements are made, you know which people need to know. You can determine who will pass on information to team members at all levels.

LEADERSHIP TRAINING

A department head doesn't need the same training as the division head or the vice president. A teacher doesn't need the same training as a department head. A senior pastor doesn't need the same as a youth pastor. Your chart helps you see which positions need the same training and which positions need different levels of training.

TRANSITION

Reorganizing a team can create major instability and insecurity. The board, the senior executive, and the executive team all can experience high levels of frustration during transition because of the ongoing demands of people and their needs. The transition may simply be the physical move of offices, or it may be the restructuring of staff and responsibilities.

Where you are asking people to do new things and take on new responsibilities, there is a feeling of living in two places. You are living with the old organizational structure while at the same time you are making changes into a new one.

We recently relocated our office. For a few days, half of our things were in our old office and half of our things were in our new office. Even though we knew the new was going to be better—an improvement in many ways—we were still halfway living in the old office.

Change typically comes with difficulty. People who have been around a long time grow accustomed to certain expectations. Change brings confusion. It takes time to move from the "old house" into the "new house."

An organizational chart is a key transitional tool to reorganizing your team. It helps you imagine how old relationships used to work, and how the new relationships will function.

Think of your new organizational chart as a builder would think of a blueprint. The blueprint is the ideal design, the pattern to use in building a new structure. Before making personnel changes, "practice" on a piece of paper. Create an organizational chart and use the chart to imagine how team relationships will work. Imagine person A reporting to person B. The organizational chart is a dynamic picture of how various people and positions presently relate in an organization. It pictures how a team works. Tool one in planning is a Strategic Planning Arrow. Tool two is an organizational chart.

Tool Two: Organizational Chart

An organizational chart can be upside down, on its side, flower-shaped, or circular as long as it addresses three critical questions:

1. Who is responsible for what?

2. Who is responsible for whom?

3. Do we have the right person in the right position?

When Cheryl, my wife, was the director of a woman's group, they had a daisy-shaped organizational chart. Each petal of the flower was an area of responsibility with a person responsible for the area. A daisy! But you know what? It answered the three critical questions. The daisy was adequate.

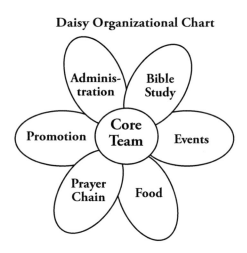

Daisy Organizational Chart

I've seen organizational charts drawn upside down to demonstrate servant leadership. A person who understands organizational charts knows that a standard chart implies a servant at the top. You don't have to turn it upside down, but if you decide to, that's fine. I've seen charts put on their side so that the leader is off to the right-hand side, providing leadership for the team. I've seen charts drawn in concentric circles, showing progressive levels.

Any chart design is fine as long as it answers the three critical questions listed above. If your chart doesn't answer the three critical questions, I don't care how good it looks, you are going to have organizational confusion.

The levels on an organizational chart indicate levels of responsibility, not levels of importance to God. Some people who are new to reading organizational charts assume that the names at the top of the chart are somehow superior to those on the bottom. Not true! It is simply a means of illustrating a higher level of responsibility. The person at the top is ultimately responsible for all others on the chart. Therefore, the higher the level, the heavier the responsibility. My friend and mentor Bill Bullard puts it this way, "The privilege of rank is sitting higher in the foxhole."

A sample organizational chart may help clarify terms. Let me go back through some of the dynamics of "charting" that might be included in your organizational chart

Organizational Chart One

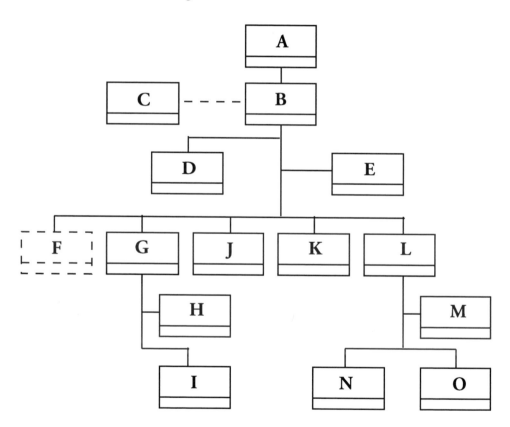

The vertical levels of your organizational chart might look like this:

"A" level might be the board of directors, deacons, elders, session, vestry.

"B" level might be the president, senior pastor, executive director.

"C" level might be a consultant, or outside agency or service, with a dotted-line relationship.

"D" level might be an administrative coordinator, which is a staff position. It is a support position for the team, but it takes responsibility for its own goal setting.

"E" level might be a secretary or an assistant. You can see how the line goes into the side of the box. It's a staff position.

"G, J, K, L" levels are line positions. They define their own priorities. Examples: worship leader, Christian education director, youth leader.

"F" level is a dotted-line box and means maybe someday, but not right away.

"H, M" levels are like staff positions, perhaps secretaries to their respective managers.

"I, N, O" levels are basically responsible to their respective managers.

The following is a sample organizational chart for a church. You don't have to organize your church in this manner. It is simply a model that you can adapt for your own purposes. However, it is critical to see that *you have the same functions and responsibilities in a church whether you have 100 percent paid staff, 100 percent unpaid staff, or a combination.* (See sample position focus sheets in Appendix C-1). Now, let me briefly explain the logic of this organizational chart.

At an essence level, in most churches you have the church board (deacons, elder board, vestry, session, etc.) with the pastor reporting to the board. Then you have six basic positions (our chart also shows a school, which is, of course, optional).

Generic Organizational Chart (Church)

```
                    ┌─────────────┐
                    │    Board    │
                    ├─────────────┤
                    └─────────────┘
                           │
                    ┌─────────────┐
                    │   Senior    │
                    │   Pastor    │
                    ├─────────────┤
                    └─────────────┘
                           │
        ┌──────────────────┴──────────────────┐
  ┌──────────────┐                      ┌──────────────┐
  │Administrative│                      │Communication │
  │   Services   │                      │   Services   │
  ├──────────────┤                      ├──────────────┤
  └──────────────┘                      └──────────────┘
```

| Christian Education | Evangelism/ Missions | Pastoral Care | Worship/ Music | School (K-12) |

Director of Administrative Services

This is a "staff/line" position. It could be a paid person in a larger church, or an unpaid team member in a smaller church. It's the person who assists the entire team with all of the administrative responsibilities. Under the director of administrative services you have each of the positions for whom s/he is responsible:

- Accounting and bookkeeping
- Computer services
- Information center
- Maintenance of buildings and grounds
- Personnel
- Purchasing
- Research
- Reception

Director of Communication Services

This is also a "staff/line" position. It is a whole new concept for most churches, even large churches. Our team has worked with a wide variety of denominational and independent churches, none of which had a communications position when we first started working with them. The director of communications services is responsible for:

- Creative services (artwork, writing, proofing, etc.)

- Fund raising (*asking* for money)

- Public relations (*telling* the church's story to the community)

- Marketing (*selling* pastoral tapes, retreat tickets, etc.)

Frequently I am asked, especially by a smaller church, "What do you mean by marketing? What would we have to market?" Many churches enjoy making their pastor's tapes available. Some have musical ensemble tapes available. Anytime you make a product available, you are selling. You want to make sure the packaging looks right, that the church name is represented properly, that copyrights are correct. Packaging something for sale is marketing. Many churches sell tickets to events. It may be the annual couples' retreat, or a sweetheart dinner, or a youth ski weekend. Any time you are trying to get people excited enough to give their money to attend your event, you are marketing that event.

Why would a church want a communications position? Let me suggest to you that there could be people in your church, especially larger churches, who work in local advertising firms. As they look around the church, there aren't very many opportunities to use their gifts and abilities. The person says, "I'm not an administrator; I don't sing in the choir; I'm not a good teacher. What I'm best at, I don't get to do at a church." By having this position on the organizational chart, and showing this to the new members class, chances are you are going to find someone who really likes marketing.

DIRECTOR OF WORSHIP AND MUSIC

- Audio/visual
- Drama team
- Greeters
- Music director (Choir, band, orchestra)
- Parking
- Special events (weddings, funerals, etc.)
- Ushers
- Worship administrator

DIRECTOR OF CHRISTIAN EDUCATION

- Cradle roll
- Nursery/toddler
- Preschool
- Elementary
- Junior high
- Senior high
- Collegiate
- Adult (men, seniors, single adults, women)

DIRECTOR OF PASTORAL CARE

- Benevolence fund
- Counseling
- Hospital visitation team
- Fellowship groups
- Pastoral counseling
- Recovery groups

- Visitation

DIRECTOR OF OUTREACH AND EVANGELISM

- Cross-cultural activities

- Evangelistic activities

- Evangelism team

- Missions (both domestic and international)

- Short-term mission trips

And then the dotted-line relationship says, "Someday we might want to have a school."

Feel free to adapt this chart to your own needs. It is a sample of one way to organize a church that has worked for many others.

You may see a close parallel between the objectives on your Strategic Planning Arrow and the positions on your organizational chart. Each objective could possibly become a position.

Note: Nonprofit organizations and for-profit corporations typically have very similar structures. You have a board of directors, a president, a vice-president of administrative services (operations), a vice-president of communications, and four to five line responsibilities. Frequently, but not always, the line responsibilities are divided by geographic distribution.

Caution: Don't design your chart around existing people. Design your organizational chart first and then identify the best person to assume the responsibility in each box.

Tool Three: A Position Focus Sheet

Position Focus Sheet

Assigned Person:_____

Effective Date: _____

1. Title of position:

2. Purpose of position: A simple statement of why this position exists.

3. Reports to: Who is this person's "team leader"? To whom is this person accountable?

4. Relates closely with: Who are the peers? Who are the other people at about the same level?

5. Responsible for: Who reports to this person?

6. Continuing responsibilities:

_____

_____

_____

_____

These are the things that are expected as an ongoing part of the day-to-day activities.

7. Primary strengths/gifts/talents required: Focus on the personal characteristics, the primary things you are looking for in the person fulfilling this position.

8. Team Profile: _____ or _____

(See Appendix II.)

9. Top three measurable priorities (goals or problems) for coming year:

A.

B.

C.

The team leader needs to determine what this position's top three measurable priorities are. When everyone involved agrees, you have just proactively avoided a lot of miscommunication and frustration in the first year. These priorities become the basis for evaluating a person's performance at year's end. Make sure that the priorities are realistic, measurable, in pencil, and remain visible.

10. Budget available: $_____

Salary is the personal remuneration you give a person for the work they have done. "Budget available" is the amount of money available to them to accomplish the tasks you have given them to perform. It is important to make this amount known to a paid staff person as well as an unpaid team member. If a person doesn't know what resources s/he has to work with, it becomes very difficult to plan.

11. Approximate salary/honorarium: $_____ per_____

An approximate amount is indicated here, knowing that there will probably be a range of salary being considered based on the candidate's qualifications.

12. Approximate time required by position:

_____hrs./week _____weeks _____months

It is critical that you clarify these assumptions. If the board is assuming that this position will require 50 to 60 hours a week, and the person is assuming it is 40, you've set yourself up for a great deal of frustration.

You also want to be very clear about how long you assume this person will be in this position—ideally! Is this a one-year assignment, or is it for five years? If you are asking someone to be a unpaid team member for the next 15 years, that's one thing. If you're asking him to take the position for the next six months, that's a very different assignment.

Caution: Be careful to word this section in hopeful terms, not promises. For example: "I sure hope you can be with us forever," not, "You have a position here forever!"

13. Benefits to person responsible: What is it about this position that is exciting, fulfilling, and encouraging? What perks come with the position? Health insurance? Vacation pay?

14. General information: Authority limits, special requirements.

    This section includes any policies that affect this position, any limitations on spending, any future considerations, any additional information you want to clarify and include in this position focus.

You don't have to adopt this position focus form, but feel free to adapt it. This tool has been used successfully by many, but to be useful it must meet your specific needs. It applies equally well to paid and unpaid team member staff.

Assignment:

Your organizational chart helps you know who is responsible for what and who is responsible for whom. Getting the right person in the right position takes two practical tools:

1. A clear organizational chart

2. The position focus sheet

It may sound complicated when you read it the first time, but your assignment is to:

❏ create an organizational chart,

❏ create a position focus sheet for each of the key positions that report to you, and

❏ get the right person in the right position.

When you've defined who is responsible for what, who is responsible for whom, and get the right person in the right place, you'll have a team chemistry that will be phenomenal. You will have the makings of an exciting, productive team.

Brain break time!

Perfect Pastors

There was a humorous chain letter being circulated, which began with a description of the perfect pastor:

Perfect pastors are 29 years old, with 40 years experience in the ministry.

Perfect pastors regularly condemn sin without hurting anyone's feelings.

Perfect pastors never preach more than 20 minutes.

Perfect pastors make 15 calls a day and are always in the office when needed.

Perfect pastors, above all, are always good looking and... a perfect pastor is always in the church across town.

The letter closed as follows:

If your pastor does not measure up, simply send this letter to six other churches that are also tired of their pastors—then bundle your pastor up and send to the church at the top of the list. In one week you will receive 164 pastors, and one of them should meet your needs.

Have faith in this letter. Do not break the chain. One church broke the chain and got their old pastor back!

CHAPTER 13

C – Cash

Brain Brander:

*When your outgo
exceeds your income
your upkeep
will be your downfall.*

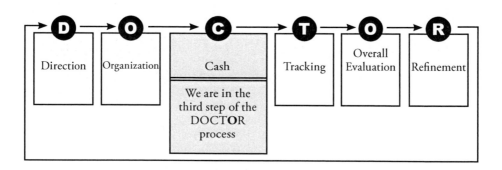

Fog-Cutting Questions:

What are our projected income, expenses, net?

Can we afford it? How can we afford it?

Chapter Overview

- Frequent Elephant Stakes
- Benefits of Understanding Finances
- A "Big Picture" Perspective of Money
- Generating Income, Controlling Expenses, Managing Reserves, Purchasing Wisely
- Financial Reporting—Thirty Minutes per Month
- Tool Four: Financial Health Checklist

Note:

From an accountant's perspective, "cash" is a very specific term. This entire section could have just as easily been called "finances."

Frequent Elephant Stakes

Elephant Stake One: "I really don't understand financial matters."

Let me assure you, I'm not trying to turn you into a CPA or a world-class expert on finances. In this section I am trying to help you gain a generalist's perspective, an overview of finances. You need to know "What should I watch as a leader?" not "What do I watch as an accountant?"

You need a basic understanding of four financial factors:

1. Generating income
2. Controlling expenses
3. Managing money
4. Purchasing wisely

To be an effective leader, you need to be generally aware of all four. If you aren't, you need to have a trusted staff member who is.

Elephant Stake Two: "I'm just not a business person."

I've been doing a fair amount of thinking lately about what it means to be a business person. I've concluded that most professional leaders aren't bottom-line business people. Seldom are doctors bottom-line business people. Professors are not bottom-line business people. Entertainers are typically not bottom-line business people.

And, surprisingly, most of the people I have worked with who own their own companies are not bottom-line business people; they are salespeople, teachers, or whatever who just happen to run a business. They frequently do not make each and every decision based on its effect on the bottom-line profit at the end of the month.

I don't have to be an expert in an area to have the basic knowledge necessary to make significant decisions for my life. Just because you are not a business person doesn't mean you can't have a certain basic understanding of money. That's what we're going to be talking about in this section.

Benefits of Understanding Finances

Accurate Financial Systems Help Keep You out of Financial Trouble

You may not be a business person, but there is a business side of your ministry. Dr. Ted W. Engstrom, former Executive Vice President of World Vision, used to say, "Any Christian organization needs to maintain a delicate balance between business and ministry. You operate within the dynamic tension of these two factors. If you think for a minute that you're not a business, stop paying your bills. It won't be long before you will be reminded that you are a business, a responsible business, even as a church. On the other hand, if you focus on profit and profit alone, your ministry will begin to suffer from that imbalance as well."

CLEAR FINANCIAL SYSTEMS GIVE YOU A CONTEXT FOR WISE FINANCIAL DECISIONS

Can we afford it? How can we afford it? If you can't answer these two questions, then you don't have a clear context to make financial decisions. You need simple systems that give you adequate information for day-to-day decision making.

ADEQUATE FINANCIAL SYSTEMS GIVE A SENSE OF STABILITY TO THE ORGANIZATION

If you don't know where you stand financially, you have no ground to build on. How much cash do we have? What are our liabilities? What are our reasonable expectations for the next month or two? Answers to these questions allow you to plan and make significant decisions concerning the future.

A "Big Picture" Perspective of Money

Let's take a look at the dynamics of a senior executive's perspective of money. The concepts presented can greatly improve your grasp of the financial condition of your organization and help you make wise, timely decisions for the growth of your team.

There is a constant, interdependent interaction with the realities of direction, organization, and cash. When your direction changes with new opportunities, when your organization changes with the addition of staff, your cash needs change as well. These three variables are constantly interacting in a dynamic organization. As you take new directions, you need more people and more cash. As you back away from projected priorities, it takes less people and less cash.

Far too many teams base their entire budget process on history rather than the future direction. Typically, we pull out last year's budget and financial statement. "Did we make our budget?" If so, we say, "Let's increase last year's budget a little and give more to this program or that program." Not for a moment do we consider where we want the overall organization to be going! We lock ourselves into a maintenance mode by confining ourselves within a budget based on last year's income and expenses, and not based on our direction.

When you enter the budget process each year, remember the sequential nature of the DOCTOR process. Begin with direction. Where are we heading? What do we want to achieve? What's most important to us? Then, look at the organization. To achieve these priorities, how large of a staff will it take? Then, and only then, do we begin to determine the budget for the coming year. Begin the budget process with a long look at your direction, organizational opportunities and needs. The cash step is third in order by design.

Generating Income, Controlling Expenses, Managing Reserves, Purchasing Wisely

These four variables need constant attention and balancing. They are the primary dynamics of a senior executive's overview of the finances.

GENERATING INCOME

There are at least four basic ways that you have of generating more income:

1. Ask for money.

   In a nonprofit organization or a church, you have opportunities to ask for funds.

2. Sell products, services, or assets.

   In a business you are more likely to trade a product or service for dollars.

   In a church context, you could sell land or buildings that you've decided not to use. You could sell tapes, notebooks, and workbooks. You can charge for some services, such as wedding coordination or building use.

3. Earn money from investments.

   Prudent investing of your reserve funds will generate interest income. Investing contributions to a building fund is better than letting it sit in a checking account with no interest.

4. Borrow.

It may occasionally be appropriate to borrow against assets. You will want to weigh the value of new or expanded opportunities against the encumbrance of debt. In most cases you don't want to risk the well-being of your current programs by borrowing too heavily. As with personal assets, it's best not to borrow or go into debt for items you can save for over a short period of time. Many items needed in a church can be funded through a short-term promotion to the congregation. People like to see a project happen and know they had a part in making it come about. Only borrow for major, long-term items that appreciate in value, such as buildings. Many people feel it is not right to borrow for any purpose. There is a lot to be said for remaining completely debt free.

CONTROLLING EXPENSES

Check your expenses regularly. This is practical and elementary! You could have a "hole in your bag" and not even know you were losing coins. Project in your annual budget what you expect your expenses will be. Then your budget becomes your guideline for expenditures and the standard by which you control your spending.

MANAGING RESERVES

Apart from placing some of your funds in interest-bearing accounts, you can also strengthen your organization a great deal by investing funds in organizational projects that have proven in the past to help you grow larger/stronger. These returns may be more effective operations (such as a new and faster computer), more people (another fund raiser on your team), and some investment that always attracts new customers/donors for your organization. In essence, you are investing some of your reserves in the growth and development of the organization itself—not just in outside investments that return money alone.

PURCHASING WISELY

Some individuals are wise about purchasing major items. They shop two or three optional suppliers, wait until sale months, and know just the right person to ask to find just the right items. Some just go pay full price!

On small items it is not that important—saving three cents on two items is hardly worth the effort. But on items you consider major (depending on the size of your organization), you can often save hundreds, thousands, or millions of dollars just by seeking a person who is a wise purchaser of goods/services. As one wise person put it, "A penny saved is a penny earned!" or as someone else said, "A penny saved is two earned before taxes!"

LISTEN TO PROVEN COUNSEL

In all areas where money is involved listen carefully to those with proven track records. Listen lightly to the one with no track record. Don't "bet the farm" either. If their counsel goes against your better judgement—wait!

You could have the best financial expert in the world come in and recommend something that seems nearly impossible. Don't give up your brain and common sense. An idea may seem right to the "expert," but if it doesn't make sense to you, don't make the investment. Keep asking questions that can help clarify the uneasy feelings you may be experiencing. Don't act on a recommendation unless you feel comfortable with it.

Financial Reporting— Thirty Minutes per Month

Depending on the organizational phase, size, and maturity of your team, the time to prepare the financial information needed for you to lead the team will differ greatly. If you are in a start-up phase, it will take a lot longer per month to gather all the information you will want. There may be less money, but there are a lot more financial decisions to be made. Once you're up and going, a large percentage of your budget is taken by recurring items which won't take much time at all (for example: A quick rule of thumb is that an established local church spends approximately 85 percent of their total annual budget in fixed expenses each year).

In a board setting it should not take you more than about 30 minutes a month to address these concerns. I've sat in board meetings where the majority of the discussion has been finances. I know the frustration of second-guessing, projecting into the dark future, debating what we can or can't do if our financial situation is maybe this or that. If a board has the essential information necessary to make its decisions, there's no need for lengthy discussion. All you need is a simple accounting system that gives you the basic information you need.

Establish an easy-to-keep, up-to-date financial report system. Keep asking yourself, "What do I *have* to know to do what I *have* to do?" If you don't have to know information on a weekly basis, just get it on a monthly basis. It will save someone a lot of time, energy, and money. If you have to know something weekly, then ask for it weekly.

FORMAL REPORTING—ACCOUNTABILITY

There is a big difference between formal and informal reports. The formal reports are for accountability, like for the IRS or your bank records.

INFORMAL REPORTING— CONTEXT FOR DECISION MAKING

Informal financial reports provide you the information needed for decision making, and no more. They give you a context for decision making, and that's their only purpose.

One day I met with the current leadership team of an organization, and the founder was there. He was a white-haired gentleman who had done well in life financially. He had some young, eager executives with him. One of them had a stack of computer reports about three inches thick. He dropped the report on the desk from just enough height that it made a considerable "thump" when it landed. Then he announced with great pride, almost arrogance, "There's the financial report!" The older gentleman sort of held his head in his hands, rolled his eyes, and pretended he had a headache all of a sudden.

I said, "Sir, I get a feeling that you may not consider that report easy reading. Do you read most of it?" He said, "I don't read any of it!" I could see the young man deflate like a pinpricked balloon. I investigated a little further: "Tell me. If you don't want to see this computer report, what *do* you want to see?" He said, "Well, if I could get a little note once a day on my desk with how much money came into the cash register, that's all I really want to know."

It was a daylight-to-dark difference between the formality of that computer printout and the informality of that little note. The older gentleman had found that in his particular business, he could make organizational decisions based on the cash that came in every day. That was the way he managed his business.

ASK FOR EXPLANATION OF REPORTS AND NUMBERS

Never accept "just data." Before you accept any financial report, ask the person who is preparing the report, "As you are preparing this report, would you make notes on any insight you have that I ought to be aware of? Keep asking yourself what this fact says to you about our organization and our financial condition."

In the preparation of the report, s/he has opportunity to catch little items that you might not have seen. Once you have people working with you on a regular basis (an accountant, a bookkeeper), if you find that they panic when you panic and they are happy when you are happy, pretty soon you trust their month-to-month judgment. But if they panic when you're happy, and you're happy when they panic, soon you see that you must go over the report yourself. You can't rely on their judgment because your judgment and theirs are very different.

MANAGEMENT BY EXCEPTION

Management by exception basically means that you take a quick overview look at the numbers in a report. As long as everything looks to be in the normal range you don't worry much about the report. But when any figure seems out of the normal range, you focus your attention, for whatever amount of time is required, on this exception. Until it makes sense to you as to why it is an exception to what you expected—keep investigating! Ask for actual numbers only when you spot a major difference between what you have projected and what the actual results are.

SITUATIONS NEEDING MORE THAN THIRTY MINUTES PER MONTH

These are situations that will require more time and attention to financial details.

START-UP PHASE

You can spend yourself into a financial hole very quickly if you have no cash reserves to back you up. Therefore you must pay very strict attention to any and all financial matters in the start-up phase of an organization's development.

BEFORE ANY "MAJOR" DECISION

You need to dig into the current financial facts before making major decisions (dollar amounts considered "major" depend on the size of the organization).

Before you spend, say 5 to 10 percent of your annual budget on some major purchase, you will want to check what the current financial realities are. It may take you a little more than half an hour to dig into the actual numbers to answer the question, "Can we afford it right now?"

Tool Four: Financial Health Checklist

It may be helpful at this point to review the following checklist of items you need to have in place to feel on top of the finances.

❏ 1. The right people are responsible for the finances. Wise outside counsel is in place.

It's critical to make a distinction between preparing financial information and making financial decisions. The bookkeeper can prepare your financial information. The accountant can prepare basic financial information, and maybe make some recommendations. But, it's the team leader or controller who basically makes the financial decisions.

Neither the senior executive, staff, or board has the time to stay on top of the financial details, nor should they. Someone needs to provide oversight of the finances. You need the right person to be in charge of the money and the right financial team to work with her/him.

With a well-selected financial officer and finance committee, you still lack the objectivity that an outside group can bring to you. Having an outside firm review your systems and records adds credibility to your financial team. Frequently, an outside firm will make helpful recommendations for handling your monies more efficiently.

❑ 2. Appropriate internal checks and balances are established.

Ideally, you need at least two people watching the money, not just one person. You don't want to present an opportunity for temptation, or for accusation. Guard the organization's financial integrity at all costs. If there are appropriate checks and balances in handling your monies, no one can accuse your staff of financial impropriety. This accountability in a church is typically between a financial officer and a finance committee.

Ideally, you need two people present when counting cash to verify the total to be deposited. You need to have different people involved in depositing funds and disbursing funds. You need a third party reconciling the amount deposited and the funds disbursed. Everyone is protected in this arrangement. A finance committee can meet, prepare the budget, and make recommendations to the board.

A WORD TO THE WISE!

The following is not to frighten you in any way but to help you understand the need for checks and balances, even in a church setting. In the past few years I have seen two church treasurers embezzle $30,000 and $40,000, respectively. A district treasurer embezzled approximately $600,000 over a six- to 10-year period of time. These were not sleazy-looking characters twisting sinister mustaches, with deep criminal histories. These were "trustworthy, Christian, praying people"—the ones least likely to embezzle anything! These were just good people in need of money; people who had no checks and balances and got tempted to cross the line. Having appropriate checks and balances is a critical key to financial integrity.

❏ 3.   Budget is established.

❏ 4.   Cash flow projections are completed.

Based on the monthly trends of the past three years of income and expense, and any significant changes to the budget as compared to the past three years, what do you project your income and expenses to be in any given month this year? The answer to this question allows you make realistic financial decisions based on "cash flow projection." A review of the past three years helps you identify the seasonal trends in income, expenses, and end balances on a daily, weekly, monthly, or as needed basis.

If your three years of financial data are not accurate, your projections will be inaccurate. You can be in trouble and not even know it. Your projections may be right on target, but you're way off base in reality. Assuming you can set up a valid projection to begin with, your cash flow projection will provide a perspective allowing good financial decisions. If you have three to five years' history, in most organizations you can begin to set up valid cash flow projections.

In a typical church, your income and expenses are not typically a straight line. One-twelfth of your annual budget is not an accurate picture of a month's income and expense. On a graph, the income may be very high in the fall season, around Christmastime. January through April will typically show a decrease from December. The summer months will be the lowest. The income graph line will rise and fall throughout the year.

Monthly projections should be adequate for most situations. A large organization that is dealing with weekly budgets in the six-figure range may need weekly projections.

A graph of expenses rises and falls with each season just as income does. Some months are predictably higher than others. Unfortunately, income and expenses don't tend to rise and fall together. If you can project your monthly income and expenses based on experience, you can make future decisions with confidence even during financial downtimes. Cash flow projections let you anticipate the seasonal variations. Plan to set aside funds during the better months to help cushion the low months.

❑ 5. Income statements are completed.

Prepare a monthly income and expense statement that reflects current financial status compared to budget year-to-date.

❑ 6. Balance sheet is completed.

Prepare an overview of your total assets, liabilities, and capital, usually on a monthly basis.

❑ 7. Annual report is completed.

Summarize your year-end financial status, indicating in graphs and charts your primary sources of income and expenses. Show the year-end statistics compared with the past few years and projections of the next few years, indicating any noteworthy trends. Report on the progress and overall health of the organization. You may also want to project your dreams and priorities for the coming year.

❑ 8. Charts, graphs, and summaries are established.

Nothing is meaningful without a context. A single graph summarizes pages of data and allows you to gain an immediate "big picture" of your financial condition.

A graph or chart helps you visualize data within a defined context. An income report is not meaningful without a comparison against what was expected or needed. The same is true for expenses.

Some people prefer numbers to charts. For others, "one chart is worth 10,000 numbers."

When you are working with visionaries, give them visuals. Visionaries tend to think conceptually, thinking of the future and leading the team. Visionaries like visuals. Looking at five sheets of visuals for three minutes will show visionaries how they're doing faster than three hours of looking at the numbers.

Instead of giving the board a thick computer report, hand them about 10 charts. Have someone present who is prepared to answer any detailed questions with hard data. One mark per month on a chart changes the entire financial context for decision making!

Put together a chart or a graph reflecting the budgeted incomes and expenses against the actual monthly incomes and expenses. Trends will be quite visible with a line graph showing the financial condition throughout the year. When this chart or graph is in place, each month you only have to add a short line to the graph to visualize each new month's progress. Each month is a new report, but all you did was add one dot and a very short line.

If your trend line has been going up for months and all of a sudden it drops 30 percent below your projection, stop and take a serious look at the reasons. The income is down, the expenses are up, so you stop spending for a while.

Key ratios are frequently extremely helpful. A ratio is simply how two numbers interact. For example: What is the income per member of the church, or how many giving units are there compared to potential units?

A *financial problem* is the distance between where you projected you would be and where you actually are. One afternoon I was sitting in the office of a senior pastor of a very large church. When the pastor came in, he had panic in his eyes. His very first statement to me was not, "Hello, Bobb," but was "Bobb, we are $50,000 in the red this month alone!" My response seemed to puzzle him when I simply asked, "Compared to what?"

"Compared to what? I said we are $50,000 in the red this month!"

I assured him that I had heard him the first time, and repeated my question, "Compared to what? If you had projected that you would be $100,000 in the hole, you are in great shape; if you had projected $50,000 down, you are right on target; if you had planned this to be a break-even month you are in trouble. So, compared to what?"

"Oh," he responded, "We had projected about $46,000 down."

I assured him that a $4,000 difference for a church his size was not significant for this time of year, and we went back to our normal discussion.

If your financial reports reveal a negative balance, but that's where you projected you'd be, you're probably not in trouble. If you have been in a similar financial condition at this same time of year for the past three years, but three months later you always moved into a positive balance, you can have reasonable confidence that you will do it again. You are where you projected you'd be. If you projected you'd have $50,000 in the bank, and you have $50,000 of bills you haven't paid, then you are in trouble. There's a big difference between your projection and reality.

❏ 9. Financial policy is defined.

Policy is what we always do or never do. Financial policy is what we always do or never do when it comes to money.

It sounds simple, but the board or the senior executive needs to set some financial policy on which everyone agrees. "We pay our bills within 30 days. We don't borrow more than X percent of our net worth," are two examples of policy or premade decisions.

Setting policy helps maintain consistency in an organization. Policy helps people know what monies can be expended under what conditions, with what authority, to what extent. Any team leader on your staff should know the process and policies in securing secure funds for an activity or project.

It takes careful "think time" to set wise policy. The highest level of leadership wisdom must be the source of policy for the team. Most financial policy is set within an organization at a board level.

❑ 10. Authority limits for each staff member are established and communicated.

The board, or senior executive, needs to set a limit on the amount of money (budgeted and unbudgeted) a staff member can spend without approval from someone else. You want everyone on your team to know what they can or cannot spend.

- Each staff person's limit may vary from that of other staff members.

- Each person's limit likely will increase over time.

Let's say a new team member could spend $100 without getting additional approval. Five years later the same team member may be authorized to spend $1000 or $5000 within budget, without checking with anyone. The trust that the leadership team has in each member will grow over the years with an accumulation of wise decisions.

Each staff person should know her/his limit from the first day of employment. As a part of orientation, new team members need to be told what their spending limit will be. Tell the new member something like, "When you are representing our team, you can spend up to $500, if it's budgeted, without asking anyone. Beyond this amount, you need to check with the finance committee or vice-president of administrative services. This limit may increase with more years of experience and established credibility."

If a board doesn't establish limits, a naive team member can make financial commitments that the team can't keep. Let's say a new staff member saw a piece of property s/he liked and told the owner of the lot, "We'll buy that lot from you. I know it's a good deal." S/he goes back to the team and the team doesn't want the lot. They can't afford it. Whose problem is it? The team member made the commitment, but it's the board's problem now. The integrity of the entire organization is at stake. As far as the property owner is concerned, the new staff member was representing the entire organization when s/he made the unwise, unauthorized verbal commitment.

Assignment:

As a summary review, check the following list and see how many of the items you have in place for your team.

❑ The right people are responsible for finances. Wise outside counsel is in place.

❑ Appropriate internal checks and balances are established.

❑ Budget is established.

❑ Cash flow projections are completed.

❑ Income statements are completed.

❑ Balance sheet is completed.

❑ Annual report is completed.

❑ Charts, graphs, and summaries are established.

❑ Financial policy is defined.

❑ Authority limits for each staff member are established and communicated.

If you have these things in place, you're pretty well on top of the cash section of your Strategic Plan. If you don't have any of these in place, the negative consequences are predictable. Use this as a checklist to make sure your financial house is in order.

Before we move on to the Tracking section, let's summarize where we are in the DOCTOR process.

✓ Your Arrow is filled out.

✓ Your organizational chart is complete, and your position focus sheets are filled out for each person reporting to you.

✓ Your financial information has been put in a notebook.

Chapter Overview

- Frequent Elephant Stakes
- Benefits of Consistent Tracking
- Tracking Assumes Priorities Are in Place
- Tool Five: Team Report—Six Reporting Questions
- Written Reports
- Staff Meetings/Team Reports

Frequent Elephant Stakes

ELEPHANT STAKE ONE: "WHY WRITE OUT A COMPLEX REPORT? I'LL STOP BY IN PERSON."

A written report documents your progress. It helps you remember what you have done. At the end of the year, you can look back and say, "We've made major progress!" Plus, it reduces miscommunication.

"Well, I thought I told you that!"

"No, you didn't tell me that."

"Well, here, I gave you the report."

"Oh, yes, I forgot! Okay."

ELEPHANT STAKE TWO: "MY STAFF MEMBERS WON'T TURN IN REPORTS ANYWAY, SO WHY ASK?"

If your staff doesn't give you a report occasionally, you can't help them win. You don't know where they are. This is a critical dimension in being a strong support to your staff and to strong progress in achieving your own priorities.

ELEPHANT STAKE THREE: "FRANKLY, I DON'T KNOW WHAT TO PUT IN A REPORT."

In most every work environment there are six profound questions you can ask to get the information you need to be a strong help to your staff. These six questions will be presented and explained in detail. Keep reading.

Benefits of Consistent Tracking

BENEFIT ONE: INCREASES CLEAR COMMUNICATION AND REDUCES FRUSTRATION

One of the most frequent concerns expressed by our clients is the lack of clear communication, internally as well as externally. Any place where there are people working together, the problem of communication exists. Frequent staff feelings include, "Well, everybody knows but me!" or "Why didn't someone tell me?"

Regular reporting builds a bridge over which two-way communication can happen. The team leader knows what the staff person is thinking and doing, and the staff person has opportunity to get input from the team leader.

BENEFIT TWO: INCREASES TIMELY DECISIONS

When the facts are clear,
the decisions jump out at you.
—Dr. Peter F. Drucker

Most decisions are postponed due to the lack of information. When reporting is taking place, information is flowing and decisions can be made.

BENEFIT THREE: INCREASES PERSONAL CARE

You can't help your staff if you don't know what they need! Reporting is a vehicle for expressing concerns, needs, wants, and suggestions. The right questions will allow you to know and demonstrate concern for your staff. When people know you care, they respond with loyalty.

Tracking Assumes Priorities Are in Place

The cross-country runner can't measure her/his progress if s/he doesn't know where the finish line is. The soccer player can't do anything more than run around kicking the ball if s/he doesn't know where the goal is. When you have a finish line, or a goal, you can focus your energy and *measure your progress.*

The primary focus of your team needs to be on your 90-day to one-year priorities! Keep asking the team, "How are you coming on your 90-day priorities?"

An article I wrote for the Christian Management Association focused on the high value of tracking your progress toward your goals through regular reporting. The remaining sections in this chapter are an excerpt from the article, "Servant Leadership Series: Reporting/Tracking."

Over 2000 years ago Jesus said (very roughly paraphrased): "He who would be the greatest team leader is to be the servant of her/his team." As a team leader, you are responsible to help your staff members achieve their priorities. You are responsible to serve them by:

- giving them clear-cut decisions;
- helping them remove the problems or roadblocks keeping them from their priorities;
- helping them make realistic, well-thought-through, achievable plans;
- encouraging them as they pass key milestones;
- being aware of their personal life so that you can stand with them in the low spots and celebrate with them when they are feeling "on top of the world";
- praying for them.

As a servant-leader, you serve those you lead in these ways. A few years ago I asked a friend, Si Simonson, who is also a nationally known efficiency expert, "What is the most helpful question you know?" He hesitated approximately one inefficient millisecond and then nailed the heart of the issue with this profound answer, "What do you *have* to know to do what you *have* to do?"

As a servant-leader, what you "*have* to know to do what you *have* to do" to serve each staff member effectively, can be found in answering six simple reporting questions.

To accomplish all of the priorities we have agreed on, ask:

1. What *decisions* do you need from me?

2. What *problems* are keeping you from reaching your goals?

3. What *plans* are you making that haven't been discussed?

4. What *progress* have you made?

5. On a scale of one to ten, how are you *personally*? Why?

6. How can I be *praying* for you?

If your staff members will answer these questions for you, you can help them reach their priorities in ways that they have never before experienced. This is true at all levels within the organization.

Having a simple report such as this has multiple advantages to you:

- Clearer communications will occur (a major problem in most organizations).

- Your staff members will clarify their thoughts by committing their answers in writing.

- They will have a documentation of their progress and accomplishments.

- You will know clearly how to help them.

- You will have a clear method of telling your team leaders how they can best help your staff members.

- You will rarely be surprised.

- You will be available to your staff members and can help them on a very focused basis in an effective way.

- By having the answers in writing, you will reduce the miscommunications that often result from differing assumptions.

If you don't know what's going on with your staff, you can't help them reach their goals, and you can't serve them. Ultimately, you can't lead them.

Tool Five: Team Report—
Six Reporting Questions

Name_____ Date_____

TO REACH MY PRIORITIES ON TIME...

1. I need a *decision* from you on the following items:

    The resource called, "Thirty Questions to Ask before Making Any Major Decisions" (see Appendix E-3) is a helpful aid in your decision making. If you are facing a decision alone, unable to discuss it with someone else, these questions help provide an objective perspective on the decision. If you'll pretend that I am sitting there with you, asking you each one of these questions, it will help bring objectivity.

    The third question has been particularly helpful to many: "Am I thinking about this decision with a clear head, or am I fatigued to the point where I shouldn't be making major decisions?" Vince Lombardi said, "Fatigue makes cowards of us all." And I add, "It causes us to be introspective and negative."

    If you are tired you will tend to back away from challenges that otherwise you would find exciting. You'll tend to doubt yourself, and you'll tend to become negative about people, life, yourself, your family, and everything. So if you're fatigued, one of the most important things to do is to rest. And, help your fatigued staff members get some rest too!

2. I am having a *problem* with the following in reaching my goals:

    When it comes to problem solving, one of the major things you want to do is to be able to brainstorm new options quickly. The resource, "Brainstorming Questions" (see Appendix E-2), can help. These questions will help you think about your problem in a variety of new contexts and enable you to see brand new solutions. This is a very powerful tool when it comes to problem solving.

3. I am *planning* to do the following:

The "Strategic Planning Work Sheet" (see Appendix B-5) helps your staff members prepare properly before bringing you any major plan. What you want to know from the people reporting to you is what they're planning to do that you *have not* agreed on. This prevents surprises. This question falls under the leadership principle, "Never surprise your team leader." What if your youth pastor says, "We want to increase attendance in our Junior High program, so we have offered brand-new, $500 bicycles to every kid who brings someone." You had better know about this plan before he commits to this $50,000 outlay by the church!

4. I have made *progress* in the following areas:

   Include financial and numerical results here. Charts and graphs are helpful. As your team meets and shares the progress, you have an opportunity to encourage each other, congratulate each other, and say, "Position well done!"

5. I would rate my *personal happiness* at _____. (1="I'm suicidal" and 10="I'm feeling on top of the world")

   This exercise helps bring objectivity to very subjective feelings. As a rule, people know what 1–10 means. I've found that even a 10-year-old child can relate to a simple scale of 1–10. Most adults feel pretty comfortable with it, but you may want to use some other rating scale. I would say 9–10 is really good; 7–8 is not so good but still okay; 4–6 is beginning to get dangerous. Anything from 0–3 you'd better check into immediately; there is the high likelihood of real trouble. You might want to explain to your staff what various scores mean to you.

6. How can I be *praying* for you? (This may be inappropriate in a secular setting.)

   Just knowing that your team leader cares enough to pray for you is very encouraging.

Written Reports

How Often Should a Staff Report?

This varies with the organization. Some want to get a written report weekly, some monthly, and some quarterly. The more complicated and the more non-routine an organization is, the more you will need to keep abreast of the progress being made.

Are Verbal Reports Acceptable?

For full-time staff, our team recommends that reports always be written. For project leaders, unpaid team member or part-time, reports can in some cases be verbal. In either case, you would cover the same questions.

Why Don't All Organizations Have Reporting Systems?

Some don't have clear priorities against which they are reporting. Others don't have an understanding of what to ask. Additionally, others seem to prefer to drift along without seeming to care that a person is "dying on the vine."

Even if your team leader doesn't ask for a written report, make a practice of submitting your own anyway. For example, give a regular report to the board telling of your progress. It will help keep the board focused on your priorities, and it demonstrates your interest and leadership.

What If One of the Staff Members Doesn't Turn in a Report?

If you don't know what your staff members are doing, you can't help them. If they will not take time to make it easier for you to help them by filling out the answers to these six simple questions once a week or so, then you need to gently insist! Unless your staff is willing to go out of their way just a little bit to give you the information you need (the decisions they need, the problems they are having), you can't help them.

Pastor Larry DeWitt told me, "You know, Bobb, I've got this one staff member who won't give me a report." I responded, "I'd make it clear to him that it is required." The next time I saw Larry, he said, "I told him, 'Because of the nature of your work and the importance of our regular communications, next Wednesday I need one of two things on my desk. Either a report, like every one of the other staff members is turning in, or your resignation. One of those two pieces of paper I need on my desk next Wednesday.'" Now that's the extreme. Most people don't require that kind of ultimatum, but he got his report. If your staff doesn't tell you what decisions they need or how they need help, you can't help them!

WHAT REACTION CAN BE EXPECTED AS I INTRODUCE REPORTING FOR THE FIRST TIME?

You will typically find that reactions fall into one of three categories:

1. Relief and appreciation (that you care)—80 percent

2. Fear of failure (from a lack of confidence)—15 percent

3. Rebellion (against any "authority")—5 percent

Staff Meetings/Team Reports

Frequently I am asked, "Which of these questions should we cover in my one-to-one time with a staff member?" and "What should we cover in staff meetings?"

Looking carefully, you will see that the six reporting questions break into two types of questions:

1. Personal—better discussed one-to-one

2. Public—better discussed in a group

The *personal* questions include:

A. Decisions

> What decisions do you need from me to keep moving toward your 90-day goals?

> You may have a person on your staff who needs a decision from

you related to her/his department only. For example, "Can I get another piece of computer hardware?" You may bore the rest of your staff while you discuss that hardware equipment for an hour. The more you can cover decisions one-to-one, the better. If the decision involves another person, then bring that other person into the discussion, but don't take group staff time for decision making or problem solving.

B. Problems

What problems are you having?

Use the same basic logic as decisions needed.

C. Personal

On a scale of one to ten, how are you personally?

This is a very personal question. You want to make sure that you've got a private enough environment for them to respond candidly. Most will respond positively, but under pressure some will confide struggles known only to them and their family. Unless you know they're hurting, how can you help them?

The *group* questions (the things to discuss in staff meetings) include:

A. Plans

Sharing plans can increase cooperation, cut costs, and minimize inefficiency and scheduling conflicts. Two or three members of your staff may plan to attend a conference 100 miles away. By sharing plans, your staff members can split the expense and chat productively during the travel time.

B. Progress

This is so your staff can very appropriately pat each other on the back.

C. Prayer requests

Invest some time praying for one another (if it is appropriate in your organization).

Do staff members ever directly communicate with their team leader's team leader? Ideally, team leaders will turn in copies of their staff members' reports with their personal reports to their team leader. If the team leader's team leader needs or wants to know a staff member's perspective on an issue, s/he can always ask to get together personally.

The best way to have staff members talk with their team leader's team leader is typically just to ask their team leader's permission. Conventional wisdom says, "Never go around your team leader without asking first."

Incidentally, what you need to see from your staff to serve them properly is *exactly* what the person responsible to help you win needs to see from you.

In conclusion, choose your staff members carefully. Help them define clearly where you and they want to go (priorities), then give them lots and lots of encouragement, plus whatever clarification they need to grow into mature leaders.

Remember, some day your staff members will be taking your place as you move on. Your responsibility is to prepare them to be wise and caring servant-leaders.

Assignment:

In light of the above information on reporting, decide today how each of your team members will report to you and how often you will require written reports. Communicate this to your staff as soon as it is appropriate.

CHAPTER 15

O – Overall Evaluation

Brain Brander:

*Evaluation is where your focus moves
from: "Do we look successful?"
to: "Are we making a real difference?"*

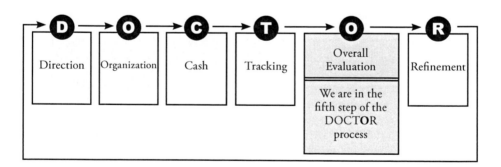

Fog-Cutting Question:

Are we achieving the *quality* we expect and demand of ourselves?

Chapter Overview

- Frequent Elephant Stakes

- Benefits of Evaluation

- Survival, Success, Significance

- Three Levels of Evaluation

- Here Comes the Mentor, Not Here Comes the Judge!

- Staff Evaluation Process

- Tool Six: Annual Staff Evaluation Questionnaire

- Tool Seven: Program Evaluation Questionnaire

- Tool Eight: Organizational Evaluation Questionnaire

Frequent Elephant Stakes

ELEPHANT STAKE ONE: "I'M JUST NOT GOOD AT EMOTIONAL CONFRONTATIONS."

Try moving from confrontation to clarification. Stop trying to *confront* someone and start focusing on *clarifying* what your perceptions of them are, where you feel they can grow, and where they want to grow. If you'll replace the word *confrontation* with the word *clarification* it will remove a lot of the emotional anxiety about the evaluation process, as well as being evaluated.

ELEPHANT STAKE TWO: "MY STAFF DOESN'T LIKE TO BE EVALUATED, SO I JUST PUT IT OFF."

May I suggest that your staff deserves, and has a right to expect, an evaluation? If you don't give them a careful, clear, well-thought-through evaluation, they don't know if they are doing well. Without regular evaluations, you will tend to give subtle clues about their weak areas. You will, even unconsciously, withhold your affection, your encouragement, or in some way try to subtly tell them that they are doing the wrong thing and hope they catch the clue. Your staff will begin to feel more and more uncomfortable. If you sit down once in a while and give them a very candid, honest evaluation, it takes a lot of fear out of the evaluation process. If you can approach your evaluations with the attitude of "I'm coming to help you" rather than "I'm coming to judge you," your staff will resist evaluation less. Make the effort to provide evaluation *before* trouble starts. Regular evaluation will help avoid big problems.

Elephant Stake Three: "They think they are being disciplined."

Occasionally discipline is necessary, but let me suggest that 80 to 90 percent of all of your evaluation should be focused on the positive—what they're doing *right*, not what they're doing *wrong*. Sometimes you have to work at it, but focus first and primarily on what they are doing right. An evaluation is meant to help a person look good, not to make them look bad. Evaluation is more *preventative* than *corrective*.

Benefits of Evaluation

Benefit One: Increases Quality—Deepens Personal Work Satisfaction

If you hear people saying, "My work just isn't as satisfying as it used to be" or "My relationships aren't as satisfying as they used to be," the key underlying the feeling of satisfaction or dissatisfaction is *quality*. When you improve the quality of what you do, it will feel much more satisfying. When you're evaluating, seek to improve the quality of your relationships and the quality of the production or service of the one you are evaluating.

Benefit Two: Provides an Appropriate Pressure Escape for Expressing Negative Feelings—Reduces "Blowups" and Turnover

If you don't give your staff an opportunity to appropriately release their pressure, they are going to talk behind your back. They will inappropriately vent their frustrations about you and your leadership style to others on the team. This is why it's appropriate and important to regularly have a time of positively balanced evaluation.

Survival, Success, Significance

Evaluation is where a team moves its focus from success to significance. Healthy evaluation moves your team from a success orientation of "Did we accomplish our priorities?" to "What difference did achieving our priorities actually make? Did we achieve the quality that will really make a difference over time?"

An organization or a person tends to be focused on one of the three phases:

1. Survival

2. Success

3. Significance

Survival people ask questions like, "Will I ever make it? Will I survive?" Some leaders you know are in the process of asking, "Will I even make it as a leader? Will our organization make it to next year? Will we be able to keep the doors open?" This is a survival focus. Frankly, it becomes very self-centered.

Success asks questions like, "Yes, we are going to make it. Now, how big can we make it? A bigger church, more staff, more buses, more this, more that? Do we look successful?" Again, the focus tends to be self-centered, although it's more of a positive self-centered attitude. It isn't an anxious, fearful self-centeredness, but it's still, "How big can *we* become?"

Significance asks questions like, "Did we really make any difference that will last? What difference will we actually be making 100 years from now? Is our product or service of the highest quality we can possibly deliver?" Significance is other-centered. Significance is the focus of the evaluation step.

Three Levels of Evaluation

A. Staff evaluation

You want not only to evaluate your staff, but also to have your staff evaluate you. Objective evaluation is always helpful—if it is committed to building the person and helping each person reach her/his full potential over the years.

B. Program evaluation

Are our programs helping us meet the needs we care deeply about? Is the quality we think is there really there?

C. Organizational evaluation

Are we achieving the quality we expect because we have the right people in the right place?

Here Comes the Mentor, Not Here Comes the Judge!

To many young leaders, the word *goal* equals failure and the word *evaluation* equals anxiety. When we hear there's going to be an evaluation, our less secure emotions cry out, "Oh no, the judge is coming!" That is not really what evaluation is all about. I'd like to try to remove some of the fear from the evaluation process. As our consulting associate Terry Fleck expresses it, "It isn't the judge that's coming, it's the mentor, the teacher, the coach, or the helper that is coming to help me."

Staff Evaluation Process

Staff evaluations tend to be very subjective. It is easy to lose an objective perspective when it comes to people with whom we work closely. The following process will be extremely helpful to you as you seek to provide an objective evaluation. (See chart on page 153.)

The first thing to ask is, "Can we leave her/him where s/he is?" If the answer is yes, then give that staff member a clear position focus and clear priorities. Regularly evaluate her/his performance. Is the person happy, productive, successful?

The following is a sample Annual Staff Evaluation Sheet. I recommend that you fill it out for each of your full-time staff members. This can be done in two ways:

1. You can fill it out as the team leader.

2. Have each staff member complete one for themselves, while you complete a separate one about them. Get together in a retreat setting and compare notes. They may think that they are doing a great position in an area where you think they are really struggling, or vice versa. On the back of the sheet you can write down your assumptions about their strongest points, where you'd like to see improvement, and what future training you recommend.

STAFF EVALUATION PROCESS

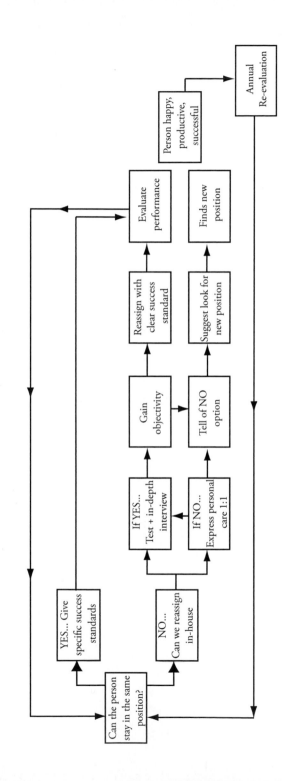

Tool Six: Annual Staff Evaluation Questionnaire

Name_____Department _____

Appraisal Period: From: _____ To: _____ Title: _____

A REVIEW OF PERFORMANCE FACTORS

Unsatisfactory	Needs Improvement	Competent	Above Requirements	Distinguished
❑	❑	❑	❑	❑

(Rate each Performance Factor on the above scale)

1. Quantity of Work: ❑   ❑   ❑   ❑   ❑

   Evaluation of the volume of work   Comments: _____
   accomplished in relation to   _____
   standards, regardless of quality.   _____

2. Quality Of Work: ❑   ❑   ❑   ❑   ❑

   Evaluation of performance in   Comments: _____
   meeting established position   _____
   requirements, accuracy, judgment, _____
   and neatness.   _____

3. Knowledge/   ❑   ❑   ❑   ❑   ❑
   Technical Ability:

   Evaluation of how much is   Comments: _____
   known about present position and _____
   the skills necessary to do it.   _____

4. Creativity/Initiative: ❑   ❑   ❑   ❑   ❑

   Evaluation of performance in   Comments: _____

   overcoming difficult situations _____

   and producing new thoughts and _____

   constructive changes. _____

5. Learning Ability: ❑   ❑   ❑   ❑   ❑

   Evaluation of ability to learn   Comments: _____

   new methods and concepts, to _____

   apply new knowledge, and retain _____

   information. _____

6. Dependability: ❑   ❑   ❑   ❑   ❑

   Evaluation of whether you can   Comments:_____

   consistently depend on the _____

   team member to perform duties _____

   within the limits of her/his _____

   experience and training. _____

7. Cooperation: ❑   ❑   ❑   ❑   ❑

   Evaluation of general attitude   Comments: _____

   toward work and company, and _____

   ability of team member to work _____

   efficiently with team leader and _____

   other team members.

Summary

Strongest Qualities

_____

_____

_____

_____

Qualities Most Needing Improvement

_____

_____

_____

_____

Suggested Future Training and Development

_____

_____

_____

_____

General Comments and Overall Performance

_____

_____

_____

_____

_____

_____   _____
Date Given   Interviewer

_____   _____
Team member Signature   Reviewed By

The evaluation forms and questions in this section are for you to utilize. You can adapt them. You can copy them. They are for your use.

At the annual reevaluation next year, ask, "Can we still leave her/ him where s/he is?" or "Do you want to serve another term?" (Use the "Building" interview questions listed below if you like.) If the answer continues to be yes, then help her/him continue to be successful and fulfilled in her/his position.

Questions to Ask in an Annual "Building" Interview

Annual staff evaluation day could actually be called "annual career path day." This is the day you ask your staff about their plans for the future and ask how you can help them get where they are going in life.

Once a year, I like to sit down with my staff in an unhurried environment without interruptions, where I can explain the purpose of the meeting and go through some evaluation questions. The basic, overall questions are, "How can I help you win? Where do you really want to grow personally this year? How can I help you grow in those areas?" There are 21 questions I use (see below). Sitting down with your staff and asking these questions will help your staff feel they are important to you. They will feel your care and concern. You will understand your staff better. Your relationship will be strengthened. I think you will find this exercise very helpful.

Notes:

- Give your team members a copy of these questions a week or two before your meeting so they can think through their answers and come prepared to discuss them fully.

- Discuss these when unhurried.

- Prevent interruptions; meet out of the office if appropriate.

- Explain, before the session, that the meeting is meant to be a building time.

- Remember, *how* you say something is often more important than *what* you say.

- Follow up with a memo documenting agreement, plans, priorities, and actions.

Questions

1. Where do you really want to grow personally this year? How can I help you grow in these areas?

2. What do you feel is holding you back in any aspect of your life? How can I help you?

3. What do you plan to do this year that you have never done before and are anxious (concerned) about doing?

4. Is anything heavy on your shoulders from outside of work that you would like to talk with me about as your friend?

5. Is any area of your life unresolved that you have been hoping to speak to me about, but the right time has never arrived?

6. What has been your most meaningful experience this year?

7. What tools, equipment, facilities, or personnel could help you most in maximizing your potential?

8. What is the single area of your life that you would most like me to help you with this year?

9. In what area would you like to see me, your manager, grow this year? What suggestions would you give me or whom would you recommend to help me?

10. What do I do that motivates you?

11. What do I do that de-motivates you?

12. What would be most helpful for me to know about you, to truly understand "the real you"?

13. What are your dreams for the next five or 10 years? If you could do anything you wanted, what would you do? How can I help in this area?

14. What do you consider your three greatest strengths? How can I help you to maximize them?

15. What courses would you like to take, what books would you like to read, and what experiences would you like to have to help you grow this year?

16. What, in your work, gives you the most personal fulfillment? Why?

17. What three people do you enjoy being with the most? Why?

18. What do you do just to have fun?

19. What, in your work, causes you the most personal stress and frustration? Why?

20. What do you feel are my expectations from you?

21. What have I forgotten to ask you that would be most helpful to me in understanding who you are, what you would like to become, and where you are going? How could I help you the most in getting there?

Let's say you ask the question, "Can we leave her/him where he/she is?" and the answer is, "No, we can't. There has to be a change." Then you have to ask, "Can we reassign her/him in-house?" If the answer is, "Yes, we can," then you might want to do some tests or some in-depth interviews to gain objectivity on what the person would rather do. Reassign the individual with a clear success standard and provide regular evaluation of performance and satisfaction.

Prior to releasing a person from a position or your organization, the following sample memo may be helpful to you, with some adaptations. My personal assistant had a typist working for her who really wasn't working out. In an attempt to communicate the situation, she drafted this memo. It clearly communicates, "There is a clear standard that you are not meeting. If you can't meet it, you cannot remain in the position. We love you. We care for you. You have great strengths. You can make it."

Date:

To:

From:

I want simply to give us both a written summary of our conversation on Tuesday, so that no uncertainty or misunderstanding on possible future events will occur.

The following points were made in our conversation, as I understand them:

1. We care for you and are cheering for you! You are a hard worker and

have a wonderful attitude. To have you in our office is a pleasure.

2. Because the workload will be increasing substantially in the near future, typing speed becomes a major concern. Therefore, your typing speed must be 60 WPM by April 1. (Anything less, although close, will not be acceptable.)

3. If this speed is not reached by April 1, then April 1 is your last day as an team member of Masterplanning Group. (This gives you 60 days to prepare.)

4. In the meantime, if you anticipate that you may be leaving, we want you to feel free to pursue another position. If you should need to take time off work for interviews elsewhere, please feel free to do so. I will give a good reference to any future employer.

We are all here to help you win!

At the annual evaluation next year you ask, "Can we leave her/him there?" If the answer is no, and there are no other options in the organization, then you express your personal care for the individual one-to-one. Explain that there really are no options for her/him to stay in that position. Suggest that s/he start looking for a new position. Provide references and possible positions that would be more fitting to the person's ability and interests.

Tool Seven: Program Evaluation Questionnaire

Note: The questionaire is for use in evaluating a program or activity. This is a simple sample that you can adapt any way you like. If you ask the right 10 people to take 10 minutes and fill out this form you will get 50 to 80 percent of the information you need to improve the program next year.

EVALUATION SHEET FOR THE _____PROGRAM

Occasionally it is important to stop and take a careful look at any program or service. We would deeply appreciate your taking a few minutes and sharing with us your feelings and thoughts on the above program. Thank you in advance for your cooperation.

1. What do you like best about the program?

2. What suggestions do you have about how we could improve the program?

3. How do you feel that you are growing personally as a result of the program?

4. Do you feel totally comfortable bringing friends into the program? Why?

5. Is there anything about the program which is upsetting to you?

6. How do you feel about the leadership that the program has received?

7. How do you feel about the direction in which the program is headed?

8. What three things could we do in the next 90 days to improve the quality of this program by 50 percent?

(Please use the back of the sheet for additional comments.)

Your Name _____Date _____

Tool Eight: Organizational Evaluation Questionnaire

Every organization's evaluation questionnaire will be unique, tailored to its specific priorities and departments.

CONGREGATIONAL EVALUATION

The following evaluation is a sample of an organizational questionnaire for a church. You will find another sample in Appendix F-2.

CONGREGATIONAL EVALUATION OF MINISTRIES AND PERSONNEL

Circle the number that best reflects your opinion. Leave blank any items that refer to areas with which you are not familiar. Please put additional comments on the back.

1. How do you think a visitor to our Sunday morning service views our church?

Our church is:	Cold/impersonal	1 2 3 4 5 6 7 8 9	Warm/friendly
Their time with us was:	Wasted/pointless	1 2 3 4 5 6 7 8 9	Meaningful/ valuable

2. Should our Sunday morning service be focused more on reaching unbelievers or on encouraging growth in believers? (5=what we do is just right)

Believers	1 2 3 4 5 6 7 8 9	Unbelievers

3. How would you rate the overall format of our Sunday morning service? (5=just right)

Too formal	1 2 3 4 5 6 7 8 9	Too casual
Too predictable	1 2 3 4 5 6 7 8 9	Too unpredictable
Too long	1 2 3 4 5 6 7 8 9	Too short

4. How would you rate the use of music in our Sunday morning worship? (5=just right)

Praise choruses:	Too little	1 2 3 4 5 6 7 8 9	Too much
Hymns:	Too little	1 2 3 4 5 6 7 8 9	Too much
New songs:	Too little	1 2 3 4 5 6 7 8 9	Too much

| Guitar group: | Too little | 1 2 3 4 5 6 7 8 9 | Too much |
| Special music: | Too little | 1 2 3 4 5 6 7 8 9 | Too much |

5. How would you rate the pastor's sermons in each of the following areas:

Impact on your life:	Minimal	1 2 3 4 5 6 7 8 9	Significant
Biblical content:	Too little	1 2 3 4 5 6 7 8 9	Too much
Application:	Too little	1 2 3 4 5 6 7 8 9	Too much
Illustrations:	Too little	1 2 3 4 5 6 7 8 9	Too much
Delivery (clarity, holds attention, etc.):	Poor	1 2 3 4 5 6 7 8 9	Excellent
Length:	Too short	1 2 3 4 5 6 7 8 9	Too long

Specific comments would be helpful to our pastor:

_____

_____

6. How would you rate the church's overall effectiveness at meeting the needs of each of the following groups? (Please add comments on the back with reference to any particular ministries or events, such as Sunday school, youth, men's breakfasts, etc.)

Children ages 0–5:	Poor	1 2 3 4 5 6 7 8 9	Excellent
Children ages 6–12:	Poor	1 2 3 4 5 6 7 8 9	Excellent
Jr. high school:	Poor	1 2 3 4 5 6 7 8 9	Excellent
High school:	Poor	1 2 3 4 5 6 7 8 9	Excellent
College:	Poor	1 2 3 4 5 6 7 8 9	Excellent
Post-college singles:	Poor	1 2 3 4 5 6 7 8 9	Excellent
Women:	Poor	1 2 3 4 5 6 7 8 9	Excellent
Men:	Poor	1 2 3 4 5 6 7 8 9	Excellent
Young families:	Poor	1 2 3 4 5 6 7 8 9	Excellent
Older families:	Poor	1 2 3 4 5 6 7 8 9	Excellent
Widows/elderly:	Poor	1 2 3 4 5 6 7 8 9	Excellent

7. Should our church schedule more or less of the following activities? (5=no change)

Social activities:	Fewer	1 2 3 4 5 6 7 8 9	More
Group retreats:	Fewer	1 2 3 4 5 6 7 8 9	More
Bible studies:	Fewer	1 2 3 4 5 6 7 8 9	More
Discipleship/ accountability groups:	Fewer	1 2 3 4 5 6 7 8 9	More
Prayer fellowships:	Fewer	1 2 3 4 5 6 7 8 9	More
Other: _____	Fewer	1 2 3 4 5 6 7 8 9	More
Other: _____	Fewer	1 2 3 4 5 6 7 8 9	More

8. How involved should our church be in each of the following areas? (5=no change)

Community (homeless, orphans, elderly, crisis pregnancy, etc.):

Less involved   1 2 3 4 5 6 7 8 9   More involved

Home/foreign missions (evangelism, discipleship, church planting):

Less involved   1 2 3 4 5 6 7 8 9   More involved

Political/moral issues (abortion, pornography, homosexuality, etc.):

Less involved   1 2 3 4 5 6 7 8 9   More involved

Other: _____

Less involved   1 2 3 4 5 6 7 8 9   More involved

9. How have the following areas of your life changed over the past year?

Personal worship:	Worse	1 2 3 4 5 6 7 8 9	Better
Personal Bible study:	Worse	1 2 3 4 5 6 7 8 9	Better
Personal prayer life:	Worse	1 2 3 4 5 6 7 8 9	Better
Sharing your faith:	Worse	1 2 3 4 5 6 7 8 9	Better
Sense of personal growth:	Worse	1 2 3 4 5 6 7 8 9	Better
Family relationships:	Worse	1 2 3 4 5 6 7 8 9	Better
Personal friendships:	Worse	1 2 3 4 5 6 7 8 9	Better

10. The church attempts to encourage growth in believers' lives by providing input (teaching, counseling, encouragement, accountability, etc.) and opportunities for output (use of gifts, serving others, etc.). With this in mind, how would you evaluate the church in each of the following areas? (5=just right)

Input into your life: Too little   1 2 3 4 5 6 7 8 9   Too much

Output expectations: Too little   1 2 3 4 5 6 7 8 9   Too much

11. If you had a personal problems how likely would you be to go to someone in this church for help with that problem?

Unlikely   1 2 3 4 5 6 7 8 9   Likely

12. How would you evaluate our pastor in each of the following areas?

Teaching: Poor   1 2 3 4 5 6 7 8 9   Excellent

Counseling: Poor   1 2 3 4 5 6 7 8 9   Excellent

Leadership: Poor   1 2 3 4 5 6 7 8 9   Excellent

Specific comments would be helpful to our pastor:

_____

_____

_____

13. How adequate are our facilities in each of the following areas?

Auditorium: Inadequate   1 2 3 4 5 6 7 8 9   Adequate

Classrooms: Inadequate   1 2 3 4 5 6 7 8 9   Adequate

Nursery: Inadequate   1 2 3 4 5 6 7 8 9   Adequate

Fellowship hall: Inadequate   1 2 3 4 5 6 7 8 9   Adequate

Other: _____   Inadequate   1 2 3 4 5 6 7 8 9   Adequate

14. If you were to meet with the church leaders and tell them your biggest concerns about our church, as well as the things that encourage you most about our church, what would you say?

Biggest concerns (3 to 5):

_____

_____

_____

Biggest encouragements (3 to 5):

_____

_____

_____

Thanks for your input! Please help us evaluate this survey by providing the following additional information:

Age: __ 8–11   __ 12–17   __ 18–29   __ 30–39   __ 40–49   __ 50+

Years as a Christian: ___ 0–1   ___ 2–5   ___ 6–10   ___ 11+

Years in this church: ___ 0–1   ___ 2–5   ___ 6–10   ___ 11+

QUESTIONS TO HELP IN EVALUATING CHURCH OBJECTIVES AREAS

Individual spiritual growth:	Are we growing in understanding, faith, practice, service?
Assimilation development:	How are we doing at involving new people in the church family? Is our membership free to participate in serving?
Leadership development:	Is every believer using her/his gift(s) in this body? Is everyone learning what they need to know to serve well?
Facility enlargement:	Are all our facility needs being met?

Personal evangelism:	Have all of our acquaintances been introduced to the gospel?
Communication:	Do you know what's going on at [church name] in its various ministries? Who's doing what? How can you get involved?
Organizational structures:	Are we organized to maximize our resources and opportunity?

Assignment:

Schedule your staff, program, and organizational evaluation dates for next year—today!

CHAPTER 16

R – Refinement

Brain Brander:

Never recreate the wheel,
but
never stop refining the tire!

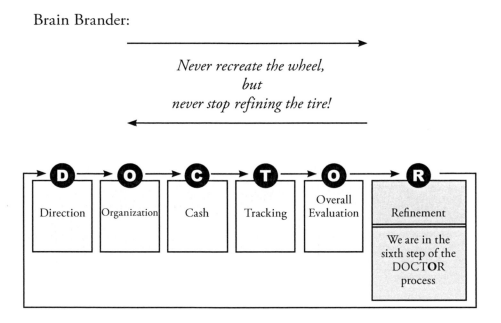

Fog-Cutting Question:

How can we be more effective and more efficient in moving toward the ideal?

Chapter Overview

- Frequent Elephant Stakes
- Tool Nine: A Process Chart
- Primary Benefits of Processing
- Creating a Process Chart

Remember, we are in the sixth and last step of the DOCTOR process. Once you have a clear *direction*, have your *organizational* team put together, and are monitoring your *cash* properly, you have your Strategic Plan. *Tracking* makes sure you are getting the results you want, and *overall evaluation* makes sure that your people and programs are developing in quality. Based on your evaluation, you notice a need for *refinement*. This is where you get to the "R" step, the refinements. Year after year you refine anything that needs changing in direction, organization, cash, tracking, or evaluation.

Frequent Elephant Stakes

Elephant Stake One: "We can't afford the time to refine our systems."

This is like saying, "We can't afford the time to fix a tire that is slowly going flat." It slows up the car, ruins the tire, and ultimately will stop the automobile. If you can't take time to fix the tire, sooner or later you will have more severe problems.

Elephant Stake Two: "We don't have any competition. We're doing Okay!"

One way to keep competition away is to keep doing a better and better position. If you don't have a competitive organization within 10 miles of you, then keep increasing your quality. They'll tend to stay away. But if you don't do the position, another organization will come in saying, "This is an area where no one is really doing the position. We can do it!"

Elephant Stake Three: "I get bored and want to move on."

Some people want to move on to the "new thing" all of the time. At the end of your life, realizing that you started and then abandoned many new projects won't be as satisfying as sticking with a few projects and doing them right.

Tool Nine: A Process Chart

One of the most effective ways to refine something is to complete a process chart, which pictures the entire process in logical sequence from beginning to end. (See sample process chart on page 169) The process you are learning from this book, the DOCTOR process, is a series of steps necessary to develop a Strategic Plan. Each step is an essential part of the process. Each step is in sequential order. A process chart shows each step in the correct relationship to all of the other steps.

In the DOCTOR process, the DOC steps are the fundamental building blocks of an organization; and the TOR steps keep the organization moving forward. This is an appropriate picture of the relationship of these business dynamics. Refinement makes the picture complete by circling back to *direction* with any modifications necessary to keep moving forward.

Process charts are also called "flow charts." They also have a very similar appearance to a "pert" chart. A process chart differs from a pert chart in that a pert chart typically describes a one-time project. The process chart is repeated time after time. If we were going to send a deep-space probe to Jupiter, we would probably develop a pert chart: "We're going to do this one time, and that's it." The process chart is more like the space shuttle program. We launch the shuttle, orbit the shuttle, bring it back to Earth, reevaluate it, and launch it again. The same craft may go up into space many times and land again. The looping (up into space, landing, reevaluation, up into space, landing, reevaluation, up into space, landing, reevaluation) is the process that it goes through.

In any organization there are many such loops. A new visitor comes to the church. What happens next? Then next? How do they qualify for membership? How do they get involved in teaching, and then how do they...? Hundreds or thousands of people will go through these loops in the lifetime of the church.

Finances represent another process. When someone puts a dollar into the offering plate, what is the process of handling the money properly? You remove the offering from the bag or plate, count it, put it in a certain kind of bag, take it to the bank, get the receipt, and give a year-end giving report.

What are the 10, 15, or 20 steps involved in processing the money? Or processing a new visitor? Or processing a cradle roll member? Or processing a new board member? This is called processing—identifying sequences that you will follow time and time again. The more refined your processes, the more effective your organization can be. (Two samples of church visitor assimilation processes, in checklist form, are in Appendix G-1.)

Primary Benefits of Processing

Once you have a process chart in place—all the pieces are identified and lined up in an appropriate sequence—then you can develop the following based on that process chart:

POLICY

This is what we always do or never do at this step in the process. For example, we never have one person count money alone, to protect her/him and to protect us.

PROCEDURE

You can determine the steps involved in completing a project. What are the steps necessary in counting and accounting for our money? How is each done?

PROBLEM SOLUTION

The process chart helps you identify the cause of the problem, not simply soothe the symptoms. Let's say you discover that some money is missing. Look at the process that the money goes through. Did the check get counted? Did it get recorded? Did it get to the bank? By looking at the process, you can find out where the problem developed.

Predicts Impact

A process chart can help you determine how a major influx of activity will impact each of the pieces of the process. What if we received an extra 50 members? Could we process all of them? You can look through the steps of your process and see where the impact would break down your system.

In 1973, I designed and developed a Love Loaf program for World Vision. It's a money container in the shape of a loaf of bread. You may have had the program in your church or seen one at a checkout counter somewhere. It has raised over $50 million for world hunger. We developed a 42-step process for producing and using the Love Loaf. We began imagining, "What if we suddenly received 1000 orders? What would we do?" It turned out that there were only two or three places in the process that would be major roadblocks and cause the system to break down. We spent a few weeks just correcting those two or three blocks in the process. In only three years, we went from start to hundreds of thousands of loaves a year, and the system never "red-lined" one time. It never broke down because we had anticipated all of the flow-through. That's what I mean by predicting impact.

Efficiency

Creating a process chart of a task or function in your organization gives you the perspective necessary to work out the fastest and best method of doing each step. It helps you do things right.

Efficiency is doing things right,
and
effectiveness is doing right things.
—Dr. Peter F. Drucker

You can become more efficient at every step. "How can we do it better, faster, quicker?"

EFFECTIVENESS

Are you doing things right? "Is this order of events the most effective way we can get the task done?" Focus on priorities in the correct sequence. You can ask, "What if we exchanged steps 10 and 13? Would that be a more effective way to process? What if we eliminated step 10?"

STAFF COMMUNICATIONS

Your process chart makes objectivity easy because it gives an overview. Once I had the Love Loaf 42-step process on the wall, whenever Ted Engstrom (who was the executive vice-president of World Vision at that time) came into my office, I could always show him exactly where we were. I could point out exactly where a problem was developing and what solutions we were exploring. When a new team leader for the Love Loaf program arrived, she was able to gain a quick understanding of the program by looking at the 42-step process chart. When our vendors came in, we could show them how important they were. If their step didn't work, then the other steps couldn't work.

CURRICULUM

Looking at the chart helps you see what needs to be taught to people at each step. Everyone doesn't need detailed training in the whole process. "What do we need to teach at each of those 42 steps?"

CHECKS LOGIC

The chart allows you and others to see the sequence and spot obvious problems. When I had those 42 steps on the wall, I had other people who were systems oriented come in and look at it. I'd explain what we were going to do, and then they could look at it and say, "Well, Bobb, why don't you eliminate step 16? I don't think you need that." It was a great logic check.

REFINEMENT

Asking good questions at each step improves the process. Ask, "How can we refine each of these steps, making them better?"

Key to Transferability

If you're transferring a program, you need a process. When I turned the Love Loaf program over to Pat Chavez, we sat down and reviewed a notebook that had the 42 step process, policies, procedures, samples, resource people—everything she needed for the Love Loaf program. I sat down for two-and-a-half hours and taped my explanation of the process. I handed her the tape and said, "Look, I designed and developed this program from scratch. It's my baby, and I don't want it to get off the track. Even though I am leaving World Vision, I want you to feel free to call me day or night." She never had to call. It took only two-and-a-half hours to transfer a multimillion dollar program to another person. That is transferability!

Creating a Process Chart

We've talked about the benefits of a process chart. How do you make one?

Steps to Creating a Process Chart

There are six basic steps or guidelines to follow when designing a process chart.

1. Start at the end.

   Establish your purpose, then work backwards. Take a large horizontal piece of paper and write your desired end result on the far right. On the far left, write the first step necessary to obtain the result for which you are looking. In between the first step and the end result, place all the steps necessary to achieve the result you want. These steps will be in sequential order.

2. Focus on "What is next?" not "How?"

   "What Next?" is what you want to focus on in a process chart, not "How?" In drawing the chart, don't try to explain how you process the money. Try to focus on what you do next.

3. Slip technique.

   What are the 15 to 40 steps that a donated dollar bill goes through in the money process at church? Let's say, for example, you have five people who have been working on the money processing. Give each person a stack of three-by-five cards (or *Post-It* Notes) and say, "What are all the steps involved in processing the offering?" One will say, "Taking it to the bank." Ask them to write that down in the past tense, "Taken to bank." Someone else says, "Well, we have to count it." Write, "Money counted." Someone else says, "Well, you have to enter it into the general ledger." "Amount entered into general ledger." "We have to give people receipts at the end of the year." "Money receipted at the end of the year." You get these cards together at a big conference table or on the floor, and lay out the cards in sequence. Once the sequence has been established, the process chart can easily become a basic checklist like this:

❏ Money counted

❏ Amount entered into general ledger

❏ Taken to bank

❏ Money receipted at the end of the year

4. Indicate monitor points.

You can put little red dots (or whatever you want) on the process chart to show what the real key monitor points are. For example, at the end of the counting, you may want to give a slip to the financial officer, saying, "This much money came into the offering." Once it's at the bank, you have to monitor how much was actually deposited.

5. Always show circularity of the system.

You want to show that the shuttle went up, but that it also came back. The money was given, but a thank you also went back at the end of the year.

Any system can be divided into a generic model of four basic building blocks:

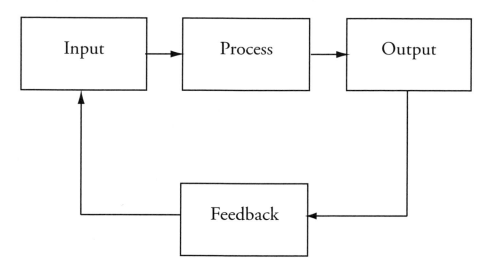

The following chart demonstrates various applications.

	Input	Process	Output	Feedback
Church	Money coming in	Accounting services	Ministry	You gave money for us to take the kids to Mexico. Here is the result. Would you like to give us more for a new project?
NASA Shuttle	Build rocket	Launch	Orbit	Return to earth and relaunch.
Refinery	Drill for crude oil	Refine	Motor oil	Test the oil's viscosity and report to the refinery how to adjust the process to increase the viscosity.

	Input	Process	Output	Feedback
Steel mill	Mine iron ore	Refine	Steel	Test for strength. Report to refinery how ore or refining needs to change to produce stronger steel.
University	Freshmen	Four-year program	Graduates	Interview alumni to see how the program needs to be more practical in the fields after graduation.

6. Evaluate the process based on the red/yellow/green test.

   Take the steps of your process and, as a team, sit down and say, "Is step one a red, yellow, or green?" Green means it's working fine, no problems. Yellow means it doesn't work quite right. Red means it has major problems; it doesn't work. You can red/yellow/green your whole process quickly as a group. In evaluating any process, always start at the left and work to the right. Focus on the yellows or the reds. Reds and yellows early in the process will be the source of other problems later in the process. If you can correct a red in step 10, then it's likely steps 11, 12, and 13 will experience major improvement as well.

KEEP THE PROCESS VISIBLE

Once you have developed your process chart, keep it visible and accessible.

- Constantly look at the forest—the process. It's an ever-present look at the whole—for example, the whole money process.

- Reduce and carry the process chart with you. On a single piece of paper you can have the essence of any program or activity.

- Hang the process chart on the wall at work. The process chart becomes a constant reminder of where you are today in the process.

It reminds you what to do next and helps you anticipate problems.

- Bring the process charts to all planning sessions. When you are talking about, "How can we improve the money-handling process here at the church?" you want to have it available so your bookkeeper, your pastor, and your board members can see what the steps are and how to improve the process.

WHAT TO DO WHEN YOU HAVE NEVER CREATED A PROCESS CHART BEFORE

Most people haven't. Now is the time to start. Let me tell you, the first few times I did it, I threw away several drafts. It seemed awkward. But the more you work at designing a process chart, the more comfortable it becomes.

Create the process chart in private first. It doesn't have to look fancy or professional. As the process chart works, then you can show it to others.

Frequently, in a complex process, I will do as many as five to 10 drafts. It's not uncommon to say, "It seems like this might...No...That works. Well, no. It doesn't really work that way; it works this way!" I've found that once you show a completed process chart to the team that has been working on pieces of it, they say, "Oh! Is that how it all fits together?" Or, when you get it done, you show it to them, and they say, "Well, yes, but where is this?" Then you realize that you've forgotten a piece. It's very exciting.

Don't let the process chart scare you. It is only a few lines and squares around your thoughts. But it can help you refine your basic systems and maximize your effectiveness and your efficiency.

Assignment:

The following can help get you and your team started:

❏ Make a list of the five to 10 key process charts your organization needs.

❏ Select the three most important.

❏ Design a process chart for your top three processes.

❏ Refine as needed.

Congratulations! You've finished the DOCTOR process. In the next chapter we will cover how to keep you focused on your own priorities and keep your team motivated to accomplish the priorities you have established!

CHAPTER 17

Keeping Yourself and Your Team Focused and Motivated

Fog-Cutting Question:

How do I keep myself and my team focused and motivated?

Chapter Overview

- You Are Responsible for Three-Way Communications
- Schedule Planning on Your Annual Calendar
- Tool Ten: Annual Tracking Checklist
- Monthly Personal Planning Day
- Quarterly Staff Planning Day
- Annual Planning Retreat Days

You Are Responsible for
Three-Way Communications

"My team leader never tells me what's going on!"

"I don't know what's going on!"

"What's going on here?"

Sound familiar? Let me suggest that you take 100 percent responsibility for communication. If you wait for other people to tell you, you're going to wait a long time in some cases. See yourself in the middle of all your working relationships. (See chart below.) Take the responsibility of communicating with those above, beside, and below you on the organizational chart. If you take the responsibility for communicating, as you should, then everyone will know what's going on. Don't assume other people are supposed to communicate with you.

Communications Model

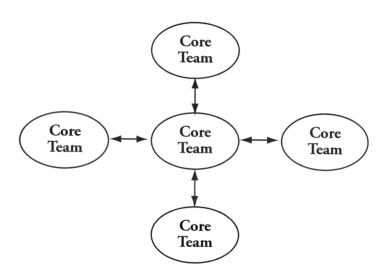

Schedule Planning on
Your Annual Calendar

It is critical when you finish reading this section to actually schedule the following planning times on your calendar for the next twelve months:

- Monthly personal planning times

- Quarterly staff planning times

- Annual planning retreat times

Schedule your planning times a year ahead so that your whole team can be prepared and arrange their calendars to avoid conflicts. Your team can also plan their work, complete their reports, and be ready to do team business. If you don't make an appointment with yourself for planning, in the rush of things you are more likely to forget.

Tool Ten: Annual Tracking Checklist

Frequently our team is asked, "How much time should one spend in planning?" Of course, the amount of time in planning will vary with the size and complexity of the organization, but there are some fundamental principles and simple models you can follow. I'd like to introduce you to the ideal in terms of annual planning and reporting. Adapt these to your own realities. You may not be able to spend as much time, or you may have to spend more time than this. Keep in mind three things:

1. Invest *up to* 10 percent of your time planning how to maximize 90 percent of your time.

   Would you agree that if you spent 10 percent of your time planning 90 percent of your work, you'd get more done on the 90 percent than you would 100 percent without planning? It isn't much at all to spend 10 percent in planning, reviewing, and communicating, especially when you consider the increase in productivity.

   20 working days per month x 10 percent=2 days per month

   ]or[

20 working days per month x 5 percent=1 day per month

2. Review and create.

Each month, review what you've already planned. If you don't have a plan, then create it.

3. Maximize your productivity and keep the communications freely flowing.

Monthly Personal Planning Time

TIME

You are responsible for scheduling your own personal planning times each year. On these days you can review your personal plans for the year in addition to your professional plans for the year. Schedule one or one-half day per month. Adjust as necessary depending on the state of projects and staff.

FOCUS:

• Keep your own personal sense of clarity, organization, and overview.

• What you are trying to do is maintain that island of clarity within your own mind in the sea of confusion around you.

• Forest-eye view.

• Day-to-day pressures can keep you focused on details. If you are to lead others, you must keep a "big picture" view. Time away from the daily routine will help you keep the "big picture" clear in your mind.

REVIEW

1. Personal Arrow

In the same way you used the Strategic Planning Arrow to find direction for your organization, you can take a personal planning retreat day away and clarify your personal Strategic Planning Arrow.

In reviewing your Arrow ask, "What are my personal priorities, and am I accomplishing them?"

2. Organizational Arrow

   Review your purpose, your objectives, your 90-day priorities, and your two-year priorities. Are you still on target? Has anything changed? Are your priorities still valid? Take a full day, if you need to, to complete your Arrow. If it is complete, just review it.

3. Organizational chart

   Review your chart. "Is there anyone that needs to change? Do we have the right people in the right places? Who else could we recruit?" Think through your organizational structure in light of your priorities.

4. Budget charts

   How are your financial trends? How are your cash flow projections?

5. Key process charts

   Are your processes of communication, production, decision making, and problem solving all functioning well, serving you well?

6. Prepare for quarterly staff planning day

   Is there anything I need to do to prepare for this?

7. Once per year, update your filing system

   Organizations tend to have busy seasons. In a church, you wouldn't want to update your filing system around the Christmas holidays, but rather in the summer. On one of your personal planning days, you may want to go through all your file cabinets and throw out all the files you don't need. Files easily get cluttered with outdated material and slow down your efforts to find materials you need.

8. Prepare a written report for your manager

   Use the six basic questions we covered on page 139.

9. Other interests or concerns

For example, you may want to update your milestone area in your Arrow with positive progress items.

10. Mark your trail. What have you learned?

What have you learned in this last month that you will want to remember? Write it down.

I picked up this phrase from the pioneer days. When they were exploring new parts of the country, they would "mark their trail." They would take a hatchet and put a notch on a tree along the trail through a forest so that other people could follow their trail and not get lost. When they returned through the dense forest, they could just follow the notches, and they'd get back to where they came from. They were "marking their trail."

As we go through life, instead of going directly and confidently from one point to the next, often we get lost in the forest and start circling. We find ourselves relearning lessons we've already learned. If you will simply write down the insights you've gained, you will soon see that you are making major progress.

Let's say I gave a talk on mentoring, and I prepared a five-page outline. When I'm done with the talk, I just throw the outline away. Two years later I want to give another talk on mentoring. I have to start over because I didn't "mark my trail." If I had kept my notes, I could have used the same basic outline, refined it, and updated it. Whatever you're learning that you don't want to forget, mark it down. Mark your trail, and the next time you're going through that particular woods, you will already have notes on it. You'll already have hatchet marks on the trees.

All right! Now you've had three of these monthly meetings (personal planning). It's time for a quarterly staff planning time. You will want to take your staff away for a day or half day.

Quarterly Staff Planning Day

TIME

Wait for your team leader to establish her/his quarterly staff planning dates. Then schedule dates for your staff one to four weeks in advance of the days with your team leader and peers. Get all the input from your staff that you can. When you go to the manager's planning day, you can report exactly what your team is thinking.

Once you have the key board meeting dates set, then you can begin backing up the planning dates of the staff or leaders of your ministries. You will be coming to the board meetings prepared, and not saying, "Our planning retreat is next week, and I don't know what my staff thinks about this." You will meet with your staff quarterly in a retreat setting.

FOCUS

Review the past quarter's progress, plan next quarter's path, keep a clear overview perspective, and plan communications with your manager, peers, and staff.

REVIEW

1. Arrows

   How is each staff member coming on her/his Strategic planning Arrow?

2. Organizational charts

3. Budget reports

4. Other reports as scheduled

5. Update team

6. Other: positive progress

7. Report to Manager

   When the quarterly planning time with your staff is done, sit down and fill out the "Six Question Report" to your team leader saying, "I just had my quarterly staff planning time. Here are some questions my staff had, some problems. Here are some decisions we need. Here are some plans we are making. Here is the progress we have made."

8. Mark your trail

Annual Planning Retreat Days

TIME

Wait for the team leader just as with quarterly days. Schedule your annual staff retreat one to four weeks in advance of the retreat with the team leader and peers, three days with staff retreat, and three days with manager and peers. Total: six days per year

FOCUS

Review the past year's progress, plan next year's path, keep a clear overview perspective. Once a year it's going to take more planning time, with all the people to report to.

REVIEW

1. Arrows

   Review and update division or department Arrows for the coming year.

2. Organizational charts/position focus changes

3. Budget projections

4. Annual reports/staff (major milestones, implications, overview of coming year's direction)

5. Program evaluation reports

6. Process refinement

7. Schedule next year's planning dates (quarterly and annual—be sure to include birthdays and parties)

8. Compare calendars, schedules (i.e., when the team leader is out, etc.)

9. Agree on the coming year's plan with your staff:

- Reporting cycle

- Staff meeting schedule

- One-on-one time

10. Other: positive progress

11. Report to the team leader progress of the staff retreat

12. Mark your trail

If you'll follow these outlines on your prayer and planning days, you'll find it makes a good checklist for your planning.

Conclusion

You are responsible for maintaining the clarity of your plans and communications only with your team leader and staff—plus your spouse!

Initially, you may be able to take only two days a month, or one day a month, or a half day a month. But do what you can do. Consider this chart:

Percentage of Days in a Year	Days per Month	Days per Year
10%	2	24
5%	1	12
2.5%	1/2	6

Schedule what you can, but schedule it today, and stay with your plan! The first year is by far the hardest. Getting in the habit of meeting regularly for planning within the various levels of your organization is difficult at first. Once you get the system in place, reviewing and planning get easier.

Remember:

*You cannot give something you do not have;
you cannot teach what you do not know; and
you cannot lead when you are lost in the forest!*

Adaptable Samples

Adaptable samples save you hundreds of hours by not having to start with a "blank sheet of paper." Adapt, not adopt, these ideas.

One Time Focus
Adaptable Samples

A-1. History Statement

Our History

The word *church* in the New Testament means "called out ones." In February 1977, God called out a small group of people to begin a new church. They met together informally from February to August for Bible study, prayer, and fellowship on Sunday evenings. The focus of their Bible study centered on the scriptural principles of the church as described in the New Testament. After much prayer and interaction, they held their first worship service on Sunday morning, August 21, 1977, at a local school. The desires which brought this original group of people together remain foundational to our church today. They are:

- A Desire for strong teaching of the Word of God

The Bible should be the foundation of all Christian experience, and the church's fundamental task is to communicate the Word of God. The teaching and preaching of the Word should be done diligently, and this demands the careful and time-consuming preparation of our pastor-teachers. Since the true worship and fellowship are founded on solid Biblical truth, the church cannot grow as it should apart from a strong commitment to uphold God's Word (Acts 6:4; 2 Timothy 3:16–17).

- A Desire to work through issues and conflicts openly and honestly

Someone once said, "To dwell above with the saints we love, oh that will be glory, but to dwell below with the saints we know, well, that's another story." When people are involved, conflicts are inevitable. Ignoring issues and conflicts compounds them; it does not resolve them. In the church, unity is not achieved in silence, but by dialogue, expression, and transparency. We are exhorted in Scripture to lay aside falsehood and speak the truth in love (see Ephesians 4:25–32).

- A Desire to apply scriptural truth to daily living

A goal of the church must be to equip people with truth for living (Ephesians 4:12). The church's ministry should challenge people with the revelation of God, not the reason of man. The emphasis of this challenge is the individual application of scriptural truth to daily living (James 1:22–25). The emphasis is on equipping rather than programming. This distinctive is shown below:

Programming Emphasis	Equipping Emphasis
Organized around events which attract people from the world	Organized around equipping which sends people into the world
Organization is the primary focus	Christian values are the primary focus
Status assigned by position in the organization	Status related to conformity to Christian values
Ministries viewed as performed by "agencies" of the organization	Ministries viewed as performed by each member of the church
Success measured by numbers, dollars, and buildings	Success measured by individual maturity and Christ-likeness

- A Desire to penetrate the community in which we live

Jesus exhorts us in Matthew 5:16, "Let your light shine before men in such a way that they may see your good works, and glorify your Father who is in heaven" (NASB). While the church is a place for developing close spiritual relationships, it is called to "reach out" to reveal Jesus Christ to the community and world in which it exists (Matthew 28:19–20). The local church should equip (Ephesians 4:11–13) its members with the message of salvation through Jesus Christ (John 14:6) and exhort them to share it in word and deed.

A-2. Needs Statement

Community Needs

1. Every person needs to get right with God.

   The lost need redemption/salvation/reconciliation

   People disillusioned with church

   People disillusioned with youth

   Hurting families/parents/partners/single parents

   Summer workers/transients/down and out/struggling

2. Every person needs to experience right relationships.

   Those at odds/empty/alone/lonely

   Families, friends, coworkers

3. Every person needs to experience the presence and authority of God in their lives.

   To have hope—a sense of positive future

   To have value—worth something to others and self

   (What is wanted is relationship, sense of value, sense of future)

4. Every person needs to pursue godly values in community life.

A-3. Purpose Statements

Three sample church purpose statements

Statement of Purpose:

> To turn *people who are distant from God* into *authentic, devoted, followers* of Jesus Christ.

Statement of Purpose:

> *Celebrate* the life of God.
>
> *Cultivate* personal growth in Christ.
>
> *Care* about one another in Christ.
>
> *Communicate* Christ to the world.

Statement of Purpose

> We exist to...
>
> Worship God
>
> Build up the believer
>
> Reach the lost

Three sample purpose statements from business

Statement of Purpose: (restaurant)

> We exist to provide the highest quality food at a reasonable price and a reasonable profit.

Statement of Purpose: (furniture chain)

> We exist to provide the average home owner with affordable furniture, provide our staff a secure standard of living, and generate a reasonable corporate profit.

Statement of Purpose: (orthopedic medical practice)

> We exist to provide the safest and most innovative medical care possible.

A-4. Dream Statements

Two sample church dream statements

1. Vision statement for our church.

   I have a dream that we will:

   - welcome the hurting, searching, discouraged, and confused in an atmosphere of joy, love, forgiveness, hope, and encouragement.

- share the good news of Jesus Christ with the residents of our area, inviting them to make a life commitment to Jesus Christ. We will use whatever means are available for this task (preaching, crusades, door-to-door, television, radio, printed page, busing, off-site Sunday schools, etc.).

- develop believers to spiritual maturity through Bible studies, small groups, seminars, conferences, camps, and retreats.

- help every believer discover their God-given gifts and talents and equip them for a significant ministry.

- be vitally involved in world missions by praying for world evangelization, by financially supporting Christian mission workers and ministries, and by sending missionaries from our congregation. We will pray for and send from our congregation hundreds of career Christian workers for worldwide service and encourage thousands of our congregation to go on mission trips both in the U.S. and in foreign countries.

- start a new church in our area every two to three years.

- provide opportunities for pastoral training for pastors who are new to the ministry and those from small- to medium-sized churches. This ministry will be carried on through internships, training conferences, and career and crisis counseling.

- be aware of community social needs and intentionally be involved in helping to find solutions and in meeting those needs.

- seek to do all this for the glory of God.

2. Our vision for someday.

  - A healthy, vibrant body alive in faith, love, and service

  - An Ephesians 4, 1 Corinthians 12, Romans 12 church

  - A church faithful in teaching God's Word

  - Eighty percent of the body functioning in ministry with joy

  - Provide ministries that meet the needs of the body

  - Provide ministries that meet the needs of the community

- Strongly related to our community

- Focused in reaching non-churched young families

- A church of 700 in two locations

- Sending our own into worldwide outreach

- Adequate staff to equip the body

Two sample business vision statements:

1. Automotive parts company

   One day we will be the largest distributor of automotive parts in our home state, in the United States, in North America, and in the world.

2. Consulting Firm

   Someday we will provide consulting services on each of the continents and make all of our primary resources available in the seven basic languages.

A-5. Core Values Lists

Two sample church core values lists:

1. Ministry distinctives and core values

We, the members and ministry team, agree together that the following ministry distinctives constitute an accurate statement of our core values. This is not our statement of faith, but an affirmation of the basic assumptions on which our ministry is to be built.

The Centrality of Jesus Christ

In every aspect of our ministry, the focal point will always be the honor and glory of the Lord Jesus Christ, the living Head of the body who is now exalted gloriously at the right hand of the Father.

The Inerrancy of the Bible

The authority for our ministry comes from the Word of God as we submit ourselves to its teaching, commit ourselves to do what it says, and yield our lives to become what Christ desires for us to be.

The Undergirding of Prayer

All that we do must have the thorough undergirding of our individual and corporate prayer support or else there can be no reason to anticipate the attending power and presence of the Holy Spirit in our ministry.

An Environment of Grace

Convinced of the absolute sovereignty of a holy God, we understand that nothing good happens in our ministry that is not the result of His grace, His unmerited favor toward us, and consequently, our ministry together must be characterized by that same grace in our response to one another.

A Decentralized Ministry

Ministry is to take place out in the midst of a fallen world, and so our challenge is to provide a balance between times when believers are gathered together to be *equipped* for ministry and times when they are sent out to do the ministry for which *every* member has been commissioned by Christ.

A Missions and Evangelism Emphasis

The conviction that Jesus Christ is the only way of salvation leads us to pursue vigorous means of proclaiming the gospel by sending our members to take the message to *all* those who need to hear, both in the local community and to the ends of the earth.

The Accountability of Small Groups

Integrity in the lives and ministries of our members requires that we provide a context for accountability relationships as we give high priority to the development of small groups where that can take place.

The Importance of the Family

Recognizing that one of the greatest battlefields and proving grounds of our faith in Christ is right within the home, we are committed to strengthening the spiritual lives of families as they seek to become beacons of light for Christ within our community.

The Significance of Humble Servanthood

Our ministry is built on the assumption that there is no task, no responsibility, beneath any of our members so that we undertake every ministry with a humble heart, grateful for the privilege of serving Christ and His body.

An Emphasis on Faithfulness, Not Fruitfulness

Rather than focus on bearing fruit in our ministries, either numerically or spiritually, we believe we are called instead to be *faithful* and allow the Lord to determine the level of fruitfulness we are to enjoy.

A Streamlined/Targeted Ministry

Although we encourage all of our members to pursue the individual ministries to which God has called them, we believe that it is better for the church as a whole to focus on a few target ministries and do them well rather than try to embrace all the ministries represented by our members.

A Willingness to Change and Innovate

We are convinced that in order to follow Christ, we must be committed to change and willing to innovate so that we do not place any barriers to growth in our way to becoming the body of believers Christ wants us to be.

These ministry distinctives provide a framework for understanding who we are and why we do what we do as the body of Christ in this location. We invite you to join with us in affirming these core values and in celebrating our life together as we grow in the grace and knowledge of the Lord Jesus Christ!

2. The values we share

The core value of our community is loving God—our relationship of love with our Father through His Son Jesus Christ, in the power of His Spirit. This relationship with our Creator is our most valuable possession and the treasure we freely offer our friends and families.

Not merely to know about Him, but actually to have a personal loving relationship with Him—to enjoy Him as our loving Father through His Son, Jesus Christ.

> *Love the Lord your God with all your passion*
> *and prayer and intelligence*
> *This is the most important command.*
> *—Jesus (Matthew 22:37–38, The Message)*

> *And this is the real and eternal life:*
> *that they may know you, Father,*
> *the one and only true God,*
> *and Jesus Christ, whom you sent.*
> *—Jesus (John 17:3, The Message)*

We share a system of values at our church that depend on the core value of loving God. Six key phrases summarize these values:

Belonging: Love. Acceptance. Community. Our daily life with Christ and one another. Strengthening families. Knowing we've been gathered together by the Father. Valuing grace, mercy, unity, peace, hospitality, and worship. "Love one another. This is how everyone will recognize that you are My disciples—when they see the love you have for each other."

Being Real: Truth. Authenticity. Shooting straight. Letting the truth about ourselves and the world pierce our heart—through the Bible, solitude, prayer, the sacraments, and one another. The truth about our rebellion and Jesus' love, sacrifice, and resurrection. Telling the truth in love. Valuing wisdom, honesty, sorrow, humility. "I am the Way, the Truth, and the Life. If you hold to My teaching, you are really My disciples. Then you will know the truth, and the truth will set you free."

Finding Meaning: Faith. Taking the leap. Conversion. Taking action based on trust and commitment. Finding meaning in the Father and the depth of His love. Valuing repentance, conversation, commitment, sacrifice, risk, chaos, foolishness, vision, dreams, and servant leadership. "Anyone who does not take his cross and follow Me is not worthy of

Me. Whoever finds his life will lose it, and whoever loses his life for My sake will find it."

Being Changed: Hope. Life change. The transforming power of the Holy Spirit. Healing the whole person. Changing from the inside out. Valuing the Holy Spirit and His work, spiritual training, accountability, teachability, faithfulness, following, hope in the eternal changes coming, beauty. "And we are being transformed into the likeness of Jesus Christ with ever-increasing brightness and beauty, which comes from the Lord, who is the Spirit."

Living Free: Freedom in Christ. To live with joy, meaning, and purpose. Free from conformity to public opinion—our identity secure in Christ. Free from the fear of death. Valuing the "law" of love, not rule keeping. Valuing simplicity, rest, work, play, families, weeping, laughing, perseverance, suffering, grace. "Christ has set us free to live a free life. So take your stand. Never again let anyone put a harness of slavery on you...The moment any of you submits to any rule-keeping system, at that same moment Christ's hard-won gift of freedom is squandered."

Giving Light: Service. Beauty. Good works. Doing justice. Loving mercy. Worship. The arts. Taking responsibility. Becoming an agent of life-change in Christ-like relationships. Using our time, energy, money, and positions. Valuing creativity, a sense of vocation, sharing Christ, involvement, caring for the poor, hospitality, mentoring.

> *You're here to be light*
> *Shine!...Be generous with your lives.*
> *By opening up to others,*
>
> *you'll prompt people to open up with...*
> *(your) Father in heaven.*
> *—Jesus (Mathew 5:14, 16, The Message)*

Two sample lists of business core values:

1. Automotive parts company

- Corporate growth each and every year
- Leadership development program for our core leadership team
- Loyalty to and from our staff
- Highest quality parts for the lowest realistic price
- Constant refinement of all our internal systems
- Annual profit

2. Orthopedic medical practice

- Compassionate bedside manner
- Push the innovation envelope within proven safety parameters
- Honesty with all patients at all times
- Continuing education for all staff to remain state of the art in our professional skills
- Firm profitability

A-6. Objective Statements

Sample church objectives:

Board

To oversee the ministries of the body of Christ, to ensure soundness of doctrine, and to maintain the biblical and practical integrity of the overall ministry of the church.

Senior Pastor

To provide directional leadership to the congregation by equipping them with a vision for ministry anchored in God's Word and leading them to grow in the knowledge of Jesus Christ through the preaching and teaching of God's Word.

Administrative Services

To provide support for the diverse ministry needs of the body through faithful stewardship, whether administrative, financial, or facility.

Communication Services

To support the ministries of the church by expanding and improving the means by which ministry needs and information are communicated.

Educational Development

To build up the body of Christ to maturity by means of instruction, teaching the Word of God, personal encouragement, and training people to walk as His disciples.

Evangelism and Missions

To take the message of the gospel to all people and nations and equip others to carry out the Great Commission.

Shepherding Ministries

To provide for the care of the total church family by encouraging Christian maturity and service to meet the spiritual, emotional, and physical needs of the body.

Music/Worship Services

To lead the congregation to experience communion with the living and holy God by providing worship opportunities which lead to a deeper awareness of His holiness, majesty, and grace.

Sample business objectives:

Automotive parts company (objectives listed alphabetically)

- Manufacturing
- Marketing/sales
- Operations
- Quality control
- Receiving/warehouse/shipping
- Research/development
- Retail stores

Direction
Adaptable Samples

B-1. Priorities Grid

To establish priorities we are answering the profound question one of my clients, Steve Douglass, President of Cru asked...

*What are the three things
we could do in the next 90 days
that would make a 50 percent difference?*

If I were to take over your responsibility today, the first two things I would do are:

1. Establish the trust of your team. Without trust I would be nowhere.

2. Make sure every person reporting directly to me had crystal-clear 90-day priorities. Using Steve's question I would ask them, "What are the three things we could do in the next 90 days that would make a 50 percent difference?"

Answer this question for each of the objective areas. As a leader, you want every person reporting to you to know precisely what you expect of them. They need to know what measurable priorities they are going to be aiming for in the next 90 days. That is a given as a part of your leadership team.

PRIORITIES GRID				
	90 Days	**One Year**	**Two Years**	**Three Years**
1				
2				
3				

© 1996 Bobb Biehl -1-800-443-1976

Consider making up an 8 1/2 x 11 inch sheet of paper with the above grid. Have one sheet for each person reporting directly to you.

Depending on your leadership style, you can approach filling out the sheet three ways:

1. Tell your staff member, "Here is what I want you to do!"

2. Ask your staff member, "What are you planning to do?"

3. My preference: Tell your staff member you will be filling one of these grids out for their area and ask them to do the same. Then get together and compare notes. Discuss your options to come to an ideal, mutually agreed-upon set of priorities.

B-2. Quarterly Priorities

Church example of quarterly priorities:

Board

1. Hold full-day board retreat with emphasis on prayer and evangelism.

2. Study and report on all current ministries and programs to detect areas of need or overload.

3. Revise and approve the selection process for board.

Senior Pastor

1. Take a mission trip to teach a one-week course on Christian leadership at the Biblical Theological Seminary in Poland.

2. Hire and train a part-time staff person to direct worship support area.

3. Present a series of sermons in conjunction with the stewardship program and the revised evangelism philosophy.

Administrative Services

1. Coordinate a major campaign to retire the current building indebtedness.

2. Repair interior water damage throughout the facility.

3. Build a third playground and add mulch and sand to existing playgrounds under the supervision of the Facility Support Services Director, in coordination with the Assistant Pastor of Preschool/Children.

Communication Services

1. Develop and design visitor brochure.

2. Upgrade computer hardware and software in Communication Services.

Educational Development

1. Enlist and train adult ministries leadership teams for men, women, singles, and small groups.

2. Enlist and train a director for the middle school and high school Sunday school teams.

3. Enlist and train one lead teacher and one assistant teacher to staff each of the 80 departments in the Preschool/Children's Sunday school.

Evangelism and Missions

1. Complete and communicate philosophy of evangelism for all ministry areas.

2. Develop a planned outreach for the Floral Gardens retirement community as an evangelistic effort.

3. Restructure the Missions Ministry to bring its organizational structure into alignment with the ministry functions.

Shepherding Ministries

1. Staff all ministry teams serving the Shepherding Ministries' areas.

2. Develop workshops and ministry events to address the prayer and pastoral counseling needs of the church body.

3. Clarify all teams' and team leaders' roles and develop program descriptions for all areas within the ministry teams.

Music/Worship Services

1. Expand position for part-time instrumental director to full-time.

2. Develop a seven-person worship team for planning, execution, and evaluation for all worship services.

3. Provide live accompaniment for at least two solo/ensemble specials a month at the 9:00 a.m. and 10:30 a.m. Sunday morning worship services.

Business example of quarterly priorities:

Automotive parts company

1. Sell $ _____ in parts this quarter.

2. Open _____ new stores this quarter.

3. Generate $ _____ profit this quarter.

B-3. Short-Range Priorities

Church example of short-range priorities:

Board

1. Implement a leadership training and development process in order to cultivate potential board members.

2. Establish guidelines to ensure appropriate percentages are directed to each category of the budget (such as personnel, missions, ministries, administration, facilities, etc.).

3. Develop a five-year facility and property plan for future growth.

Senior Pastor

1. Meet weekly with Worship Evaluation Team to make continued improvements to corporate worship services.

2. Revise teaching materials for new members' assimilation in conjunction with new members' training process.

3. Develop and conduct two conferences: a Bible conference with a guest speaker for our congregation and a pastors' conference to encourage and equip pastors from other churches.

Administrative Services

1. Renegotiate copier contracts and acquire additional copier(s) to serve the needs of the ministries.

2. Implement and coordinate a three-year stewardship campaign.

3. Coordinate renovation of the sanctuary.

Communication Services

1. Coordinate the publication of a church pictorial directory to be developed in-house.

2. Design and develop, in coordination with Shepherding Ministries, a new member packet for the deacons.

3. Assist the Stewardship Ministry Team in the development of materials and publicity for stewardship emphases.

Educational Development

1. Develop and promote a 13-week Basic Christian Growth Ministry Bible study series for our small groups program.

2. Establish a new mid-week Bible study in the Singles Ministry.

3. Provide a Gospel Basics Seminar formatted specifically for youth.

Evangelism and Missions

1. Coordinate three mission trips through the Missions Ministry Leadership Team.

2. Identify three key third-world ministries and form an alliance for the exchange of personnel, teams, and ministries.

3. Initiate a four-week campaign to reinforce evangelism as a core value, with the primary aim being to help our congregation understand our evangelism philosophy and how each member fits into it.

Shepherding Ministries

1. Go online on the Internet to communicate prayer needs and mobilize worldwide prayer.

2. Develop an assimilation process to engage 80 percent of the membership in practical places of ministry.

3. Transfer responsibility for that assimilation process to the Deacon Ministry.

Music/Worship Services

1. Develop a complete sound equipment inventory list and maintenance system for all equipment on the list.

2. Recruit and develop 30 additional unpaid team members to help lead corporate worship.

Business example of short-range priorities:

Automotive parts company

    1. Sell $ _____ in parts this period.

    2. Open ____ new stores this period.

    3. Generate $ _____ profit this period.

B-4. Mid-Range Priorities

Church example of mid-range priorities:

Board

    1. Visit five other church board meetings as a way to continue growing in our approach to ministry leadership.

Senior Pastor

    1. Begin a one-year internship for young pastors with a curriculum that includes training in all aspects of being a senior pastor.

    2. Accept speaking opportunities outside of our church up to four weeks out of the year.

    3. Pursue publication of a book on Christian leadership.

Administrative Services

    1. Coordinate the replacement of the present worship center roof.

    2. Develop a written long-range plan to accommodate the space needs of the adult, youth, and preschool/children's ministries and bookstore.

    3. Coordinate planning of the new worship center and related facilities.

Communication Services

    1. Assist in development of informational materials and publicity

for new facility needs.

2. Develop a comprehensive plan for production and printing of church materials and publicity.

Educational Development

1. Develop a comprehensive ministry for accommodating approximately 300 single parents.

2 Provide leadership to four city-wide youth events involving youth ministries in the area.

3. Conduct regional Vacation Bible School in three underprivileged neighborhoods.

Evangelism and Missions

1. Initiate a two-day community-based seminar to promote racial reconciliation.

2. Develop a "faith promise" missions budget separate from the church's operating budget for all missions activities and projects and raise $ _____.

Shepherding Ministries

1. Develop a three-month internship training program in the Pastoral/Crisis Care Ministry area.

2. Sponsor a two-day "Prayer Summit."

Music/Worship Services

1. Develop a plan to send our church musicians for evangelistic outreach ministries to five Eastern European countries.

Business example of mid-range priorities:

Automotive parts company

1. Sell $ _____ in parts this period.

2. Open ____ new stores this period.

3. Generate $ _____ profit this period.

B-5. Strategic Planning Work Sheets

I was working with a campus team with an executive team in Montana. Seeing the Strategic Planning Arrow, they said, "Oh, this is incredible! But do you have a way of applying the Arrow logic to an individual project?" They were planning a weekend activity called a Senior Panic, designed for seniors who were asking, "What am I going to do now that I'm out of school?" A student was going to be assigned to plan and follow up on this activity and needed a planning tool. This Strategic Planning Work Sheet was my answer.

Let's say, for example, you are planning a couples' weekend retreat in the fall, and you've asked a couple to be in charge of it. What do you give them as a planning tool, or what do you give them as a framework for the assignment? Try using the Strategic Planning Work Sheet. Basically it's a list of questions:

STRATEGIC PLANNING WORK SHEET

What are the five needs that we will be trying to meet on this couples' weekend? Or what are five things we will have participants accomplish?

Why are we having a couples' retreat? What is the essence?

What are the three roadblocks that could keep this from being a successful couples' weekend?

What are the three key resources we bring to bear?

What specific, measurable things are we trying to accomplish as a result of this weekend?

Consider your time line and budget.

What are the major action steps or areas of responsibility like publicity, food, hotel reservations?

Who is responsible for each action step? What is their target date for completion?

How much revenue is it going to bring in?

How much will it cost? What will the net be?

After you calculate your income, expense, and net, you will have a rough preliminary budget. You might also make general notes on things that have come out of your steering committee concerning assumptions, thoughts, hopes, possibilities, and lingering questions.

At the end of the retreat, ask anyone responsible for a given project to do an evaluation. How were the facilities, the people, the food, the service?

Make some recommendations for next time. "Next year at the couples' retreat, we would recommend that you do this, or we'd suggest this, or here's how we thought we would improve it if we were to be responsible for it again."

Ask them to include samples of all materials in their evaluation for future review. Take all of the samples, brochures that promoted the weekend, registration forms, sign-up forms, everything, and put them with the Strategic Planning Worksheet in a file folder labeled Couples' Weekend. Next year, when another couple takes responsibility, they've got the documentation on all that went into the previous year's retreat—who was in charge, what tasks needed to be covered, and where they found certain resources.

I'll never forget my first assignment at World Vision. I was chosen to coordinate the annual picnic which, at the time, had about 400 people attending. I said, "Great! I'd be happy to. Could I see last year's file?" There was no "last year's file." I said, "You mean last year's coordinator didn't keep any records? Do we know who provided the food service?" "Well, no. No one kept that record." I made up my mind that year to document everything. Next year's coordinator would have a track to run on. The caterer, the games played, the overall evaluation—everything would be available.

If you completed a Strategic Planning Work Sheet for each of your two-year priorities, or your 90-day priorities, you would have a clear description of the steps necessary for completing the priorities. The Strategic Planning Work Sheets are inexpensive tools available at BobbBiehl.com. Whenever you make a major assignment, ask the person, "Would you fill out the Strategic Planning Work Sheet?" It's a planning tool that can save you time and energy and give you a focused assignment. It helps you feel like you are organized.

The Strategic Planning Work Sheet is listed here by permission of Aylen Publishing.

B-6. Speed Modeling Trips

A. *Introduction*

    1. You can learn more in two days in a speed modeling trip than you can often learn in two months in school.

        a. Same or similar work as yours

        b. Larger or in work longer

        c. Friendly and open to comparing notes

    2. Never ask/expect a competitor to teach you his secrets!

    3. Plan speed modeling trips into your schedule well in advance.

        Take a day or two per visit. Combine two or three visits to an area if your trip is overnight.

    4. Why should they help you?

        a. Iron sharpens iron.

        b. They get to "brag."

        c. They like your admiration.

    5. Cheapest consulting available!

B. *Preparing for Your Visit*

    1. Define what you really want to know.

    2. Go with a list of questions and things to share, if they seem open.

    3. Don't forget to factor in the differences.

a. Time in business

b. Size

c. Market, etc.

4. Take a recording device but ask permission before turning it on.

5. Take a gift!

C. *In Your First Hour*

1. Express your admiration, respect, and affirmation as soon as you can in good taste.

2. Assure them you are not a competitor.

D. *How to Maximize Your Trip*

1. Collect samples. Take some to share with them.

2. Take notes. It honors their answers. Ask permission first!

3. Focus on the positive, not on finding their weak areas.

   a. Awe, praise, appreciation—95 percent

   b. Suggestions you feel would be sure to help them succeed even more—4 percent

   c. Analysis/critique, if you must—1 percent

4. Assume the person needs encouragement.

5. Offer to return the favor; invite them to your organization.

E. *Warnings*

1. Be generous.

   a. Offer to pay for samples.

   b. Buy meals.

    c. Give gifts.

2. Never recruit their staff!

F. *Key Question Samples to Adapt to Your Situation*

1. What primary strengths do you feel it takes to play this role effectively?

2. What have been the *three to 10 breakthrough concepts* which have allowed you to realize the success you have?

3. What *principles or rules of thumb* have you found helpful?

4. What variables do you watch to monitor the *vital signs* of this area?

5. What do you feel are the three to 10 components in your *success formula*? Why are you as successful as you are? If you had to start over, what would you do differently?

6. What *roadblocks* are you facing today with which I may be able to help you?

7. What are the *primary resources* with which you are working— the suppliers, etc.—that may be able to reduce our costs?

8. Do you have any *forms* that you have found particularly helpful in carrying out your responsibilities?

9. Do you have any *samples* that you wouldn't mind sharing with me—such as process charts, policies, procedures, checklists, etc.?

10. Do you have *any questions* as to how we do anything that might be helpful to you?

Add your own questions as well. Go with a list of questions—don't rely solely on memory or you may draw a blank and not complete your agenda.

G. *Benefits*

   1. Remember:

      You can typically learn more in two days on a speed modeling trip than you learn in two months at school.

   2. Broader perspective

      a. New people—networks

      b. New ideas—creativity sparks

      c. New solutions—options

   3. Sense of growing instead of stagnating

   4. A list of resources to call to help resolve future problems

H. *Conclusion*

   1. Post-visit Evaluation Questionnaire

      a. Mark your trail carefully.

      b. Within 24 hours of the visit

      c. Copy to your manager

   2. Encourage your staff to take speed modeling trips.

   3. Reporting—focus on what your own team has done right and how to improve it

   4. Say thank you after you return.

      a. Your host

      b. Your manager

      c. Your team

Speed Modeling

Post-visit Evaluation Questionnaire

1. What is the most helpful insight you gained during your visit?

2. With new perspective, what are the five primary things you have concluded we are doing right and should keep on doing?

3. What are the top three things we can learn from this organization?

4. Who was your primary contact on this visit—name, address, and phone number—and what are the key things you want to remember about the person for your next visit?

5. What were your overall impressions of the image, environment, attitude, and intangible dimensions of the organization? What can we learn from these?

6. What are the three primary things you personally will do differently as a result of your visit?

7. What new needs did you become aware of that we may be able to meet?

8. Are there any new products, resources, services, models, etc., that are really winning for them that you would like to have us consider?

9. What are the top three ideas you gathered that we should keep for future use?

10. What do you now see as the top three roadblocks keeping us from reaching our full potential as an organization?

11. To summarize, what were the primary benefits to you and to our organization from this speed-modeling trip?

Organization
Adaptable Samples

C-1. Position Focus Sheets

Church Models

Assigned person: <u>Name of person</u>

Effective date: <u>Date of employment</u>

Review date: <u>Date of review by team leader</u>

(annually thereafter)

POSITION FOCUS SHEET

1. Title of position: **Senior Pastor**

2. Purpose of position: To carry out the purpose of the church by preaching the Word, equipping the saints, and shepherding the flock

3. Reports to: Board

4. Relates closely with: The body

5. Responsible for: Associate Pastor
                            Administrative Assistant
                            Ministry Leaders

6. Continuing responsibilities:

    a. To preach the Word and provide for pulpit supply

    b. To equip the saints for work of service

    c. To provide counsel and encouragement to the body

    d. To plan and coordinate church calendar
    e. To conduct weddings, funerals, and related counseling

    f. To work with board in providing oversight of ministry development and overall spiritual growth

    g. To work with council leadership in providing oversight of church operations

    h. To represent our church at denominational meetings

7. Primary strengths/gifts/talents required:

    a. Heart for God and His people

    b. Knows and applies the Scriptures well; credible

    c. Clear communicator; able to teach, encourage; visionary

    d. Church ministry experience; board qualified

    e. Seminary degree

8. Team Profile: Designer/Developer or Developer

9. Top three measurable priorities for coming four months:

    a. To increase worship service attendance from ____ to ____

    b. To increase church giving from $ _____ to $ _____

    c. To develop a written five-year church Strategic Plan

10. Budget available: $ _____ Annual budget as approved by congregation

11. Time required by position: 50 hours a week

12. Salary: $ _____ per year

13. Accompanying benefits: Social Security, medical coverage, business expenses, conference and seminar expenses, three weeks of paid vacation

14. Additional considerations: Monday will be a regular day off.

Assigned person: <u>Name of person</u>

Effective date: <u>Date of employment</u>

Review date: <u>Date of review by team leader</u>

(annually thereafter)

POSITION FOCUS SHEET

1. Title of position: **Administrative Assistant**

2. Purpose of position: To provide for the administrative needs of the church and free the pastor for effective ministry

3. Reports to: Senior Pastor

4. Relates closely with: Associate Pastor/Board/ Ministry Leaders

5. Responsible for: Office personnel

6. Continuing responsibilities:

   a. Receptionist: Answer calls and greet visitors, screen and refer requests

   b. Office Manager: Keep office functional/supplies stocked/equipment working/files accessible/work with printer, shippers, postal service

   c. Assistant to Pastor: Set up meetings and appointments/ assist with projects

   d. Communications: Produce weekly bulletin, monthly newsletter/send out guest, birthday, anniversary letters

   e. Record keeping: Maintain membership information, church statistics, legal papers

f. Project coordinator:
facilitate and track projects/
insurance, tax, ministry, facility/
coordinate unpaid team members,
calendar

7. Primary strengths/gifts
/talents required:
Relational/Organized/People-
manager/Cooperative teamplayer
Flexible/Dependable/Initiator/
Spiritually mature/Wise/Experienced
Typing skill/Knowledgeable
of office equipment/Computer
competent

8. Team Profile: Developer or Developer/Manager

9. Top three measurable priorities for coming year:

a. Update church membership data base

b. Reorganize filing system

c. Recruit assistant and publish a monthly newsletter

10. Budget available: Office budget as approved by congregation

11. Time required by position: 30 hours a week
Mon.–Thurs. 8:30–3:00
Fri. 8:30–12:30

12. Salary:
$ _____ per year
(Includes salary, FICA, Fed/
State, SDI)

13. Accompanying benefits:
Two weeks paid vacation, 10 paid
holidays, paid training/seminars, no
medical by agreement

14. Additional considerations: Agreement is valid until revised.
Both parties will provide a 30-day
notice of resignation or termination.
Termination based on ethical
or moral reasons may be immediate.

Assigned person: <u>Name of person</u>

Effective date: <u>Date of employment</u>

Review date: <u>Date of review by team leader</u>

(annually thereafter)

POSITION FOCUS SHEET

1. Title of position: **Director of Communications**

2. Purpose of position: To support the ministries of the church by expanding and improving the means by which ministry needs and information are communicated

3. Reports to: Senior Pastor

4. Relates closely with: Administrative Assistant/Ministry Leaders

5. Responsible for: Graphics unpaid team members
                              Newsletter unpaid team members

6. Continuing responsibilities:

    a. Keep overall perspective on church calendar of events.

    b. Develop and produce communication tools for church events/activities.

    c. Develop and produce communication tools for each ministry.

    d. Provide oversight of computer equipment and use.

    e. Publish monthly newsletter.

    f. Nurture "family" sense in congregation by communicating personal news.

g. Think strategically about all promotion: timing, content, image, delivery method.

h. Evaluate effectiveness of each communication tool and improve.

7. Primary strengths/gifts/talents required:

Design skills/Organization/Ability to write motivating script or copy

Strategic thinker/Motivator

8. Team Profile: Designer, Designer/Developer

9. Top three measurable priorities for coming year:

a. Design and develop a new visitor packet

b. Coordinate the publication of a church pictorial directory

c. Coordinate computer hardware and software upgrade

10. Budget available: Communications budget as approved by congregation

11. Time required by position: 40 hours a week

12. Salary: $ _____ per year

13. Accompanying benefits: Social Security, medical coverage, business expenses, conference and seminar expenses, two weeks of paid vacation

14. Additional considerations: Monday will be a regular day off.

Assigned person: <u>Name of person</u>

Effective date: <u>Date of employment</u>

Review date: <u>Date of review by team leader</u>

(annually thereafter)

POSITION FOCUS SHEET

1. Title of position: **Director of Christian Education**

2. Purpose of position: To build up the body of Christ to maturity by means of instruction, teaching the Word of God, personal encouragement, and training people to walk as His disciples

3. Reports to: Senior Pastor

4. Relates closely with: Administrative Assistant/Financial Director

5. Responsible for: Coordinators of age-level classes/small-group leaders
Superintendent of Preschool

6. Continuing responsibilities:

   a. To provide and oversee age-level classes on Sunday morning

   b. To encourage, help establish, and oversee small group ministries

   c. To provide ongoing teacher training for all church teachers

   d. To coordinate instruction between Sunday classes and preschool

   e. To keep overall perspective on spiritual health of church and instruction needed

   f. To provide instruction opportunities for all interest groups

7. Primary strengths/gifts/talents required:

   Spiritual maturity/Commitment to Scriptures/MA in Christian Education

   Relational skills/Understanding of curriculum dynamics/ Discipling heart

8. Team Profile: Designer/Developer, or Developer

9. Top three measurable priorities for coming year:

   a. Develop and promote a "Basic Christian Growth Ministry," providing opportunity for all who want to grow in their faith

   b. Develop a comprehensive ministry for single parents

   c. Conduct regional Vacation Bible School in underprivileged neighborhoods

10. Budget available: Christian education budget as approved by congregation

11. Time required by position: 40 hours a week

12. Salary: $ _____ per year

13. Accompanying benefits: Social Security, medical coverage, business expenses, conference and seminar expenses, two weeks paid vacation

14. Additional considerations: Monday will be a regular day off.

Assigned person: <u>Name of person</u>

Effective date: <u>Date of employment</u>

Review date: <u>Date of review by team leader</u>

(annually thereafter)

POSITION FOCUS SHEET

1. Title of position: **Director of Worship/Music**

2. Purpose of position: To lead the congregation in experiencing communion with the living and holy God by providing worship opportunities which lead to a deeper awareness of His holiness, majesty, and grace

3. Reports to: Senior Pastor

4. Relates closely with: Administrative Assistant

5. Responsible for: Music team/Sound team

6. Continuing responsibilities:

    a. To plan, prepare, and lead worship and music teams each Sunday morning

    b. To develop performance skills of all interested musicians

    c. To provide oversight of sound system, and expand as necessary

    d. To recruit and involve musicians in outreach ministries

7. Primary strengths/gifts/talents required:

    Heart for God and His people/Skilled musician/Arranger/ Coordinator skills

8. Team Profile: Designer/Developer or Developer

9. Top three measurable priorities for coming year:

   a. Develop worship teams for planning, execution, and evaluation of worship services.

   b. Develop a plan to send out musicians for evangelistic outreach ministries.

   c. Build an inventory of sound equipment for ministries on and off site.

10. Budget available: Worship/Music budget as approved by congregation

11. Time required by position: 40 hours a week

12. Salary: $_____ per year

13. Accompanying benefits: Social Security, medical coverage, business expenses, conference and seminar expenses, three weeks paid vacation

14. Additional considerations: Monday will be a regular day off.

Assigned person: <u>Name of person</u>

Effective date: <u>Date of employment</u>

Review date: <u>Date of review by team leader</u>

(annually thereafter)

POSITION FOCUS SHEET

1. Title of position: **Director of Missions/Outreach**

2. Purpose of position: To take the message of the gospel to all people and nations and equip others to carry out the Great Commission

3. Reports to: Senior Pastor

4. Relates closely with: Administrative Assistant

5. Responsible for: Evangelism Explosion Team Leader and Mission Partners

6. Continuing responsibilities:

   a. To develop relationship of missionaries with church

   b. To provide evangelism training annually

   c. To develop evangelistic outreach activities for the church

   d. To encourage evangelism in every ministry of the church

   e. To coordinate church participation in summer short-term missions

7. Primary strengths/gifts/talents required:

   Heart for the lost/Coordinating skill/Recruiting skill

8. Team Profile: Designer/Developer or Developer

9. Top three measurable priorities for coming year:

   a. Initiate a campaign to reinforce evangelism as a core value of church.

   b. Complete and communicate a philosophy of evangelism for every ministry area.

   c. Identify three key third-world ministries with which we can partner for the exchange of personnel, teams, ministry.

10. Budget available: Missions/Outreach budget as approved by congregation

11. Time required by position: 40 hours a week

12. Salary: $ _____ per year

13. Accompanying benefits: Social Security, medical coverage, conference and seminar expenses, two weeks paid vacation

14. Additional considerations: Monday will be a regular day off.

Assigned person: <u>Name of person</u>

Effective date: <u>Date of employment</u>

Review date: <u>Date of review by team leader</u>

(annually thereafter)

POSITION FOCUS SHEET

1. Title of position: **Pastor of Caring Ministries**

2. Purpose of position: To provide for the care of the total church family by encouraging Christian maturity and service to meet the spiritual, emotional, and physical needs of the body

3. Reports to: Senior Pastor

4. Relates closely with: The body/Women's ministries

5. Responsible for: "Care Giver" team members

6. Continuing responsibilities:

    a. To lead the church in focus on praying

    b. To establish and maintain a church prayer chain

    c. To develop and maintain a system of assimilation of new members

    d. To provide on-going training in care giving to interested members

    e. To coordinate care giving in the congregation

    f. To visit the members in hospitals, retirement homes, and confined to home

    g. To represent our church at district and national conferences, and district pastors meetings

7. Primary strengths/gifts/talents required:

   Heart for hurting people/Coordinator skills/Encourager/Mercy gift

8. Team Profile: Developer/Manager or Manager

9. Top three measurable priorities for coming year:

   a. Establish a church "Prayer Home Page" on the Internet.

   b. Develop an assimilation process to engage the entire membership in practical places of caring ministry.

   c. Develop and train a counseling team for the church.

10. Budget available: Care budget as approved by congregation

11. Time required by position: 40 hours a week

12. Salary: $ _____ per year

13. Accompanying benefits: Social Security, medical coverage, business expenses, conference and seminar expenses, two weeks paid vacation

14. Additional considerations: Monday will be a regular day off.

Business model

The development of a position focus sheet is one area in which there is very little difference between profit and nonprofit preparation. Developing a position description for a president is very similar to a Senior Pastor. Here is a look at a president's position description; you can easily see the marked similarity.

Assigned person:	<u>Name of person</u>
Effective date:	<u>Date of employment</u>
Review date:	<u>Date of review by team leader</u>
	(annually thereafter)

POSITION FOCUS SHEET

1. Title of position: **President**

2. Purpose of position: To carry out the purpose of the corporation by providing overall team leadership in reaching the corporate priorities

3. Reports to: Board of Directors

4. Relates closely with: Board and executive staff

5. Responsible for: Vice-President of Manufacturing

    Vice-President of Marketing/Sales

    Vice-President of Operations

    Vice-President of Quality Control

    Vice-President of Receiving/ Warehouse/Shipping

    Vice-President of Research/ Development

    Vice-President of Retail Stores

6. Continuing responsibilities:

   a. To provide overall team direction

   b. To hire, evaluate, and fire vice-presidential-level staff

   c. To manage the team to profitability

   d. To monitor the progress of team members on an ongoing basis

   e. To evaluate the quality of the team's results

   f. To make sure all systems are in continual refinement mode

   g. To be the public spokesperson for the corporation

   h. To bring constant innovation into the corporation within legal, moral, ethical, and safety guidelines

7. Primary strengths/gifts/talents required:

   a. Senior level of leadership skill

   b. Solid financial grasp of profitability

   c. Expert in the field of our endeavor

8. Team Profile: Designer/Developer or Developer

9. Top three measurable priorities for coming year:

   a. To increase the number of stores from ___ to ___

   b. To increase sales from $ _____ to $ _____

   c. To develop a written five-year Strategic Plan

10. Budget available: $ _____

11. Time required by position: 50–60 hours a week

12. Salary: $ _____ per year

13. Accompanying benefits: Social Security, medical coverage, business expenses, conference and seminar expenses, four weeks paid vacation

14. Additional considerations: Company car is leased for the president.

C-2. Checklist for Adding New Staff Members

→

Hiring the right person—
a round peg in a round hole of the right size.

←

Once you have your organizational chart designed you need to get the right people in the right positions. The following is the essence of the Masterplanning Group Resource called *Pastoral Search Process.* It describes how you go about hiring the right person and screening out the wrong ones. When you are about to hire someone, here are the 18 things you will want to work your way through in a prudent hiring process.

→

The best time to fire a person is before you hire them.
—Dr. R. C. Sproul, President,
Ligonier Ministries

←

❑ 1. Consult your Strategic Planning Arrow and organizational chart. "Is this the right position to add next?"

❑ 2. Appoint a search committee (optional).

❑ 3. Create a position focus sheet and a profile for the position.

❑ 4. Make sure you have budget approval.

   I've seen even seasoned leaders started talking to a person about joining their staff only to find out when s/he checked with their board that there wasn't money available.

❑ 5. Announce the position opening.

   If someone on your staff is interested in the position, s/he will appreciate the opportunity to be notified before you start seeking resumés. Run your ads, call some friends, let the position opening be known.

❏ 6. Begin receiving resumés and establish a file for each one received.

❏ 7. Send or give the basic information packet to people sending resumés.

Information packets should include the position description and general information about the position. Help the person decide whether or not s/he wants to continue pursuing the position.

❏ 8. Contact references and make sure you get a good, positive report.

I knew a pastor who said he had built a church from 100 to 300 in just two years in a small town. It turned out he was an absolute liar. He had come from a different denomination, and no one had thoroughly checked his references. He looked good. He sounded good. He was friendly. He preached well, but it took them a year or two to find out that he was a sociopathic liar. By the time he left, he had created a lot of community ill will toward the church because he had lied on so many occasions. A quick reference check will often prevent oversight like this.

❏ 9. Conduct your first interview with the person and evaluate your observations.

❏ 10. Have the candidate complete some psychological inventories and create a psychological profile.

❏ 11. Conduct your second interview and evaluate your observations.

❏ 12. Conduct your third interview and evaluate your observations.

The first interview can be deceptive, concealing who a person really is. On your first interview with the person, s/he will tend to wear her/his best suit of clothes, brightest smile, and finest manners. At the second interview, you're beginning to look at who the person is on a different level. By the third interview the candidate is relaxed enough to let you begin to see who s/he really is.

❏ 13. Provide for a trial period.

If possible, let the person try the position for a while. Do everything you can to get a feel of how s/he would actually perform. Ask the person to teach a class, preach a sermon, or lead a seminar, whatever is appropriate for the position. Conduct this trial before the actual invitation to join your team. See how s/he actually works.

❏ 14. Have a final search committee discussion and come to a decision.

❏ 15. Make an offer in writing and await their acceptance.

Don't put anything in writing to which you first haven't agreed verbally. Often an offer is made in writing, and when it isn't acceptable, you end up rewriting the proposal 15 times. Discuss and come to agreement on terms and conditions of employment. Clarify all the assumptions and expectations. Then simply confirm the discussions in writing.

❏ 16. Prepare for their arrival.

Make sure the desk, the office, and everything else is in order when the person arrives. A top executive I know went to work for a Christian organization and was greeted by quite a surprise. "Oh, was this the day you were supposed to be coming?" His office wasn't ready. He didn't have a desk yet. His phone wasn't connected. They weren't ready for him. Horrible beginning! First impressions are lasting!

❏ 17. Provide an orientation to the organization.

Put together an orientation checklist of all the things a new team member needs to know to get along well.

❏ 18. Conduct an evaluation.

The first day a person starts in a new position is the time to schedule her/his first evaluation. Whenever a new person joins your team, your first evaluation should be at the end of the first day. At the end of the day, go in, sit down casually, and ask, "How do you feel about the day?" Often you can pick up something that's been a miscommunication or a problem. If you pick it up at the end of the first day, it becomes no problem. If you don't get it that first day, s/he may go three or four days creating this bogeyman in her/his mind, only to find out that it wasn't true at all. You could have nipped it in the bud at the end of the first day.

At the end of the first week sit down and do the same thing.

At the end of the first month sit down and do the same thing.

At the end of six months do the same thing.

At the end of the year, sit down for a formal evaluation.

If s/he is a winner, you loop around and prepare to fill the next position.

Note: This entire process is spelled out in a detailed notebook and a three-hour tape series called *Pastoral Search Process* from Masterplanning Group.

C-3. New Staff Orientation Checklist

Sample one:

Orientation Process for New Staff Member

Preparation

❑ Design and coordinate orientation and training schedule to include specific ministry area elements, as well as standard new-hire information (i.e., staff leave, telephone system, office equipment, supplies/resources, etc.).

❑ Create staff planning notebook with updated staff roster and organizational chart, office and facility diagrams, appropriate ministry budgets, church calendar, and all planning schedules; provide framed staff values plaque.

❑ Create personnel file and have personal information form completed.

❏ Make appropriate changes to office suite signage, staff birthday calendar, business cards, etc.

❏ Assign phone extensions and make additions/changes to staff directory.

Orientation

❏ Welcome new staff member and make office introductions.

❏ Discuss role of Staff Director/Office Manager.

❏ Provide staff organization chart, handbook, planning notebook, etc., as detailed above in Preparation.

❏ Issue building key (if appropriate).

❏ Inform new staff member of calendar items, such as routine weekly meetings (Monday 9:30 a.m.–12:00 p.m. cabinet meeting; Monday 12:00–1:00 p.m. staff meeting and luncheon; Friday 6:30–8:00 a.m. Board meeting), and of special events and occasions, such as monthly birthday celebration and staff retreat.

❏ Conduct detailed office and facility tour.

❏ Commence orientation and training schedule:

Office Systems / Management: Provide training on telephone features and system, how to program and retrieve e-mail messages, ministry long-distance codes, extension list, receptionist/greeters (how to handle incoming calls), sign-in/out sheet and its importance, etc.

❏ *Facilities/Security:* Provide training on building keys and security issues.

❏ *Computers:* Provide training on e-mail, calendar, etc.

❏ *Supplies/Resources:* Explain procedure of requesting office supplies via e-mail and the purchasing/accounting procedures associated with those items not stocked in general supply. Special orders are available for such things to be charged to individual ministry budget accounts.

❏ *Book Distributor:* Orders placed twice each month from requests entered via e-mail. Distributor offers a variety of items at a discount, payable either from the ministry budget or personal reimbursement.

❑ *Photocopies:* Identify the small office-suite copier available for their use and have their Administrative Assistant demonstrate the operations of the large copier in the copy/supply room for larger positions.

❑ *Media:* Explain guidelines of working with Media Department and schedule training session.

Accounting: Business Administrator will explain about payroll and insurance forms. Administrative Assistant will explain about purchasing procedures and budget system.

❑ Design customized staff development plan.

❑ Establish time line for three, six, and 12 month evaluations.

Evaluation

❑ Initiate evaluation procedure on quarterly schedule at three, six, and 12 months.

❑ Oversee staff development plan and assess individual progress.

❑ Facilitate any ongoing or spontaneous training support.

❑ Compile evaluation report and follow up all resultant issues.

Sample two:

Steps to Follow in New Pastoral Staff Orientation

Keys s/he will need

❑ Position descriptions for each staff position

Procedures and appropriate forms for:

❑ business expense reimbursement

❑ dental expense reimbursement

❑ purchasing supplies

- ❏ reserving rooms for use
- ❏ reserving the VCR
- ❏ getting dates on the Master Calendar
- ❏ time of staff meetings
- ❏ policy on coffee breaks

Pastoral responsibility for:

- ❏ Sunday evening lock up
- ❏ Sunday evening announcements, etc.
- ❏ Sunday morning platform schedule

Computer operations:

- ❏ manual
- ❏ arrange for training sessions
- ❏ set up directories and passwords
- ❏ when trouble develops—what do we do?

Follow up:

- ❏ new visitors
- ❏ new converts

Visitation:

- ❏ pastoral hospital visitation policies
- ❏ pastoral visitation days
- ❏ who visits whom

Other things for new pastoral staff:

- ❏ budget and financial reports
- ❏ names of church board members and standing committees
- ❏ guidelines for the church board and duties of standing committees

❏   organizational structure

❏   list of our goals

❏   church directory

❏   staff parking procedures

❏   history of the church

C-4. Leadership Development Checklist

Description:

Create a checklist of the materials you would recommend if an eager staff person, or your older child, came to you and asked:

"Of all the materials you have read, watched, or listened to, which 10 to 20 would you most highly recommend I study to develop as a leader?"

Rationale:

1.   This profoundly simple idea is one thing you can do in *one hour of your time* to create a "Mini Leadership Development Program" for your entire staff, your family, and every young leader you ever meet—with occasional updates—over the next 50 years!

2.   This simple assignment lets your staff see that you want them to develop as leaders, not just use them as tools of your organization.

3.   This simple checklist gives each person a crystal-clear track to follow as s/he develop over the next few months and years. You have provided a track; now the onus is on her/him to take the initiative to follow the track!

Primary Advantages:

1.   *For one hour of your time* you guide 50 to 300 hours for each person who receives the list over the next 10 to 20 years!

2.   *Gives fast trackers a clear track to run on* and lets you identify the fast trackers in your group quickly!

3.   *Speeds each person's learning curve* by avoiding the thousands of

books in your library that you have read but today would not recommend to anyone.

Step-by-Step Instructions:

❏ Make a simple list of the 10 to 20 resource materials which have helped you the most in your leadership development. Include any materials you have developed. You may want to develop a supplemental list of materials from your organization as a basic staff orientation checklist.

❏ You may want to include audio/video resources as a part of the basic list or list them separately. You may also want to divide the basic list into *Required/Recommended Reading.*

❏ Sequence the list(s) into the order you would recommend they be studied. Start with the most elementary and end with the most difficult.

❏ Write a brief introductory paragraph explaining that this material is to be done "at your own pace" for "your own personal growth."

Optional Enhancements:

❏ Annotate each item, explaining why this resource is included.

❏ Stock the list in your office library for loaning purposes.

❏ Offer awards, recognition, even personal time off as incentive to complete the list.

❏ Agree to meet with staff members after they finish one to three resources and interact on three basic questions:

    a.   Do you have any questions?

    b.   Any disagreement with the author?

    c.   How will you apply the principles to your life?

LEADERSHIP DEVELOPMENT CHECKLIST

Recommended by Bobb Biehl,
President, Masterplanning Group

If my son or daughter were to ask:

"Dad, of all of the leadership development materials you have ever written, read, watched, or listened to, which 25 would be the most helpful to my personal development?"

The following list would be my recommendations (in sequence).

Materials by Bobb Biehl

❏   1.   ASKING Profound Questions – *Booklet*

❏   2.   Boardroom Confidence – *Book*

❏   3.   Career Change / Lifework – *Traction Paper*

❏   4.   Depression, Fatigue, Burnout – *DVD Series*

❏   5.   Dreaming Big! – *Book*

❏   6.   Encouraging Your Team – *Traction Paper*

❏   7.   Focusing By Asking – *Audio CD*

❏   8.   4ᵀᴴ Grade – *DVD*

❏   9.   Leadership Academy – *DVD Series*

❏ 10.   Leadership Insights – *Book*

❏ 11.   Leading with Confidence – *Book*

❏ 12.   Life Focus Sheet – *DVD*

❏ 13.   Mentoring – *Book*

❑ 14. Mid-Life Storm – *Book*

❑ 15. On My Own – *Book*

❑ 16. Phases of Your Life – *DVD*

❑ 17. Staying UP in DOWN Times – *DVD*

❑ 18. Stop Setting Goals – *Book*

❑ 19. Strategic Planning Arrow – *24" x 36" Sheet*

❑ 20. Strategic Planning Worksheet – *11" x 17" Sheet*

❑ 21. Strategic Planning – *Book*

❑ 22. Team Profile – *Self Scoring Inventory*

❑ 23. Want to be President? – *DVD*

❑ 24. Why You Do What You Do – *Book*

❑ 25. Wisdom of a Grandfather – *DVD Serie*

Start with any resource that naturally interests you or simply go from 1 to 25.

Cash
Adaptable Samples

D-1. Special Event Budget Form

			Actual Event Budget

Income:

Registrations:	Number of people	@ $___	_____
	Number of people	@ $___	_____
			_____
Sales:	Materials		_____
	Books		_____
	Display rental		_____
	_____		_____
	_____		_____
	_____		_____
Underwriting:			_____
Scholarships:			_____
		Total Income:	_____

Expenditures:

Facilities:	Number of people	@ $	_____
	Number of people	@ $	_____
	Number of people	@ $	_____

	Number of people @ $	_____
Honorariums:	Speakers	_____
	Music	_____
	Airfare	_____
	Entertainment	_____
	Staff	_____
	Nurse	_____
	Security	_____
	_____	_____
Program:	Materials	_____
	Notebooks	_____
	Staging/Decorations	_____
	Equipment rental	_____
	_____	_____
	_____	_____
	_____	_____
	_____	_____
Promotion:	Brochure	_____
	Postage	_____
	Advertising	_____
	Food	_____
	Transportation	_____
	Insurance	_____
	Committee set-up costs	_____
	_____	_____
	Expenditures Subtotal:	
Miscellaneous:	10 percent of subtotal	_____
	Total Expenditures:	_____
	Net cost to ministry:	_____

Tracking/Reporting
Adaptable Samples

E-1. Team Report

Name_____Date_____

To Reach My Goals on Time...

1. I need a *decision* from you on the following items to proceed toward my goals:

2. I am having a *problem* with the following in reaching my goals:

3. I am *planning* to:

4. I have made *progress* in the following areas:

5. Personally, I would rate my "*personal happiness*" at: _____

6. You can pray for me in the following areas:

E-2. Brainstorming Questions/
Idea Sorter Questions

Brainstorming Questions

1. What is the one-word, one-sentence, one-paragraph essence of our idea? (Many words could be substituted for "idea," such as program, project, or department.)

2. Why are we doing what we are doing?

3. What are our five most fundamental assumptions? (sequential)

4. What changes would we make if we had unlimited time/three years/three days/three hours/three minutes to accomplish this task?

5. Where will this idea be in 10, 15, 25, 50, 100, or 500 years from now?

6. What if we had unlimited staff? Half of the current staff? One or two extra people? What would they do? Why?

7. What changes would we make if we had double our current budget? Unlimited budget? Half our current budget?

8. How can we double the income and cut our costs in half?

9. Which part of the total idea warrants extra funding?

10. Which part could we drop and not really miss?

11. What is the ultimate "blue sky" potential of the idea?

12. What five things could keep us from realizing the full potential? How can we clear away the roadblocks?

13. What are our greatest strengths? How can we maximize them?

14. If we had to start over, what would we do differently?

15. What if this idea were 100 times as successful as we planned?

16. What would it take to be number one in our entire field?

17. Where will our market be in 10 years from now?

18. What 10 things do we want to accomplish in this area within 10 years?

19. How do we, as a team, feel the environment will have changed for this idea in the next 10 years?

20. In our most idealistic dreams, where will our *team* be 10 years from now?

Idea Sorter Questions (Sort your good ideas from your great ideas.)

1. Which idea best meets our needs? Meets our design perimeters?

2. Which has the highest future potential?

3. Which would be the most cost effective in the long run?

4. Which best fits our overall Strategic Plan?

5. Which is the most realistic for our staff today? Do we have the right project leader?

6. Which could help us win rather than just get by?

7. Which has the lowest front-end risk?

8. Which would work best day-to-day?

9. Which facts are still missing before we can properly decide?

10. Which is really worth the overall risk involved?

11. What are the predictable roadblocks?

12. How do our senior executive and board feel about the project?

13. Where would we get the funding to do it right?

14. Why have those who have tried similar ideas in the past failed?

15. What are the side effects, good and bad, of the idea we are considering?

16. Would I put my personal money into this project or idea?

17. Is the timing right?

18. Can we protect, patent, and/or copyright it?

19. Would we have to stop something we are now doing to take on this project?

20. How can we test the idea before committing major resources to it?

E-3. Thirty Questions to Ask Before Making Any Major Decisions

1. At its essence, in one sentence, what decision are we really facing? What is the *bottom* bottom line?

2. Have I given myself 24 hours to let this decision settle in my

mind?

3. Am I thinking about this decision with a clear head, or am I fatigued to the point where I shouldn't be making major decisions?

4. What would happen if we didn't do what we are planning to do?

5. Is this the best timing? If not now, when? Why not?

6. What difference will this decision make in 5, 10, 50, or 100 years from now?

7. Are we dealing with a cause or a symptom? A means or an end?

8. What would the ideal solution be in this situation?

9. Who, what, when, where, why, how, how much?

10. What are the key assumptions we're making? What do we assume it will really cost? What do we assume will be its real benefits? What do we assume...?

11. How will this decision affect our overall Strategic Plan? Will it get us off track?

12. Is this different direction consistent with our historic values?

13. Is this decision helping maximize our key strengths?

14. Should we seek outside counsel on this decision?

15. How do we really *feel* about this decision? (Write out your answers.)

16. What are one to three alternative options?

17. Should we write a policy about this type of decision in the future?

18. What questions are lingering in our minds that are unresolved? (list)

19. Do I have peace of mind about a yes or no answer as I pray about it and look at it from God's eternal perspective?

20. Can the big decision be broken into subparts with subdecisions made at a few go/no points along the way?

21. Is this what we would do if we had twice the budget? Half the budget? Five times as much time? One tenth the time? Twice as many staff people? Half as many staff?

22. What facts should we have before we can make this decision with total confidence?

23. As we each make a list of our top three most respected advisors, what would each probably advise us to consider in making this decision?

24. How do our spouses and families feel about this decision, if they are affected by it?

25. What does the Bible say about this decision?

26. If I had to decide in the next two minutes, how would I decide and why?

27. Have we verified what the results have been for others as they have made this decision? Have we checked references? Have we actually interviewed previous users of the product or service?

28. What trends, changes, or problems are making this change needed? (list) How long will these trends last?

29. Are we possibly hunting an elephant with a .22 caliber rifle or a rabbit with an elephant gun?

30. What are the hidden agendas? Why are we or they pushing for change? Where is the emotional fuel coming from that is driving this decision?

E-4. Crisis Management Process

Occasionally the future of the entire organization hinges on your response to a crisis. The following checklist gives you a track to run on if this should happen.

1. Pray—give thanks—check our motives—praise!
   Gaining God's perspective turns panic to sovereignty.

2. Put into "big picture" context.
   Remember the positive progress we've already made.

3. Essence question: What is the situation?

4. Turn the sensational into simple truth.

   Answer falsehood or problem with positive initiative. Move from defensive to positive position. Talk about a positive future.

5. Remember: Newspapers typically misquote.
   Love the people; assume positively.

6. Identify the legal implications.

   Be wise as a serpent and harmless as a dove.

7. Create distribution list.
   Communicate simple honesty in and concern for their well-being.

8. Identify the first three action steps.

9. Centralize the process of communications, if necessary.

10. Hold question-and-answer session with top leadership team, with open and honest update, answering their anxiety questions. Ask for their support.

Assumptions in a crisis:

1. People communicate sensationally in a crisis.

2. Newspapers sell on sensation and fear.

3. What men mean for harm, God means for good. Treat people in a Christian way, even in a crisis.

4. Focus on what this means.

5. Reduce the situation to the fewest number of working parts and concepts possible.

6. Assume we are making too much of this issue—and at the same time, that we are not making enough of this issue. It's dangerous to make either assumption completely until the crisis is past.

7. Answer questions honestly—or not at all!

8. Asking for help says, "We are on the same team."

Overall Evaluation
Adaptable Samples

F-1. Staff Evaluation Questionnaires

Sample one:

ANNUAL PERSONAL DEVELOPMENT PLAN AND EVALUATION

The following information must be completed during the planning/evaluation cycle for each member of the staff:

- Position Description:

  An accurate documentation of the current position expectations.

  The immediate team leader is responsible for creating and updating this document and reviewing with the Personnel Committee for approval.

- Position Plan:

  A written description of what the team member is expected to accomplish during the current evaluation period.

  The immediate team leader is responsible for documenting this plan within one month of initial employment or within one month after a new annual review period begins.

- Plan Evaluation:

  An evaluation based on the team member's plan, documented and communicated to the team member in a team leader-team member meeting.

An evaluation must be completed for each team member at least once each year, and may occur as often as every three months. New team members must have their first evaluation three months after their employment date. An overall evaluation will be given for the current evaluation period within the following ranges:

1. Far exceeds expectations

2. Exceeds expectations

3. Meets expectations

4. Partially meets expectations

5. Does not meet expectations

The immediate team leader is responsible for the evaluation. This "Personal Development Plan and Evaluation Form," parts 1 and 2, must be used during the evaluation process.

Section 1—Plans

The following is a review of the staff member's plans based on the major position responsibilities and the plans established for this review period. In the spaces provided below, specify each adopted plan and consider to what extent it was accomplished. Be sure to identify all factors that caused the plan to succeed or fail.

The following scale will be used to rate the degree to which the staff member met the expectations stated in their performance plan goals for the evaluation period:

1. Far exceeds expectations

2. Exceeds expectations

3. Meets expectations

4. Partially meets expectations

5. Does not meet expectations

Goal: Rating:

(List goals)   (Rate each goal)

Team leader's Summary Assessment of Section 1—Plans

Comments:

SECTION 2—RELATIONSHIP RESPONSIBILITIES AND SKILLS

The following section addresses the staff member's overall skills and the degree to which relationships that flow out of her/his work have been handled during the evaluation period.

Categories: Rating:

COOPERATION/TEAM SPIRIT

Willingness to help others accomplish their ministry objectives

FLEXIBILITY/ADAPTABILITY

Ability to be flexible in adapting to unexpected situations

COURTESY

Respect for the feelings of others and politeness on the position

STABILITY

Even temperament under unavoidable tension and pressure

INNOVATION

Imagination and creativity used to improve overall effectiveness

RELIABILITY

Dependability, responsibility, and trustworthiness

INITIATIVE

Voluntarily starts projects; attempts non-routine positions and tasks

PERSEVERANCE

Steadfast pursuit of position objectives when faced with unexpected obstacles

ALERTNESS

> Ability to understand quickly new information and respond well in new situations

COMMUNICATION

> Expresses ideas coherently and succinctly so that others can easily understand

REPORTING

> Thoroughly and consistently prepares and presents reports to team leader in timely manner

POSITION KNOWLEDGE

> Understands position and executes ministry plan without hesitation

PLANNING

> Thinks ahead and prepares appropriate plans to accomplish ministry plans

FINANCIAL/BUDGET

> Fiscally responsible and works within available budgeted resources

Team leader's Summary Assessment of Section 2—Relationship Responsibilities and Skills

Comments:

Team leader's Overall Summary (Combination of Sections 1 and 2)

Summary Comments (including strengths and suggestions for improvement):

This evaluation has been reviewed together by the staff member and team leader.

Staff Member's Signature and Date _____

Team leader's Signature and Date _____

Sample two:

PASTOR'S STAFF DEVELOPMENT PLAN*

(INFORMAL QUARTERLY REVIEW)

Review Quarter: Feb. May Aug. Nov. (circle one)

Review for: _____

Position: _____

Reviewed by: _____

Review date: _____

Last review: _____

1	2	3	4	5	6	7	8	9	10
Does not Meet Goals		Partially Meets Goals		Meets Goals		Exceeds Goals		Far Exceeds Goals	

Development Area:

Focus:	Understands position and is executing performance plan
Initiative:	Looks for ways to improve ministry area
Reporting:	Prepares consistently, plans for meetings, thorough, keeps team well-informed, no surprises
Servant-minded:	Puts the needs and desires of others ahead of himself and his own interests
Teachable:	Open to new ideas and insights, receives suggestions without being defensive
Team spirit:	Supports other ministry areas, willingly unpaid team members to assist others, seeks to

put ministry distinctives into practice, extends grace to and looks for the best in others

Work habits: Diligent, not a "clock watcher"

General Comments and Suggestions for Improvement:

Date Reviewed with Staff Member: _____

Signature: _____

*This review is not kept as part of your permanent record, but is used only as a tool to provide a progress report each quarter.

F-2. Felt Need Survey

Occasionally it is helpful to ask your staff, your congregation, or your market, "What are your felt needs today?" Once you know their needs, it is far easier to develop programs which are effective in meeting those needs.

(Strictly confidential)

Completed by: _____

Organization: _____

Date: _____

Introduction

This Felt Needs Survey is intended to help in three specific ways:

1. Helps focus your thinking

2. Helps build a communications bridge between us

3. Helps me know how to help you most

For quick reference this survey has been arranged in the following categories:

- Personal Profile

- Past Needs

- Present Needs

- Future Needs

- Free Forum

Thank you in advance for the thought and the time you invest in this project!

Personal Profile

1. I am a ❏ female, ❏ male

2. I am ❏ 20–29 yrs old, ❏ 30–39, ❏ 40–49, ❏ 50–59, ❏ 60–69, ❏ 70+

3. I am a(n):

   ❏ board member

   ❏ senior executive

   ❏ executive staff member

   ❏ member of the organization

   ❏ friend of the organization

4. I learn best:

   ❏ by attending a retreat or seminar

   ❏ by reading

   ❏ by experiencing

   ❏ by reflecting on what I have seen or heard

   ❏ by watching a video

   ❏ by watching someone model a new behavior

   ❏ other _____

5. I have the following available to me:

   ❏ cell phone

   ❏ _____

   ❏ _____

6. Personally I find that:

   ❏ goal setting energizes me and problems drain my energy.

   ❏ problems energize me and goal setting drains my energy.

   ❏ both goals and problems energize me equally.

7. In my most honest moments (neither style is right or wrong— just very different) I would identify more with a:

   ❏ surgeon -"My staff is there to maximize me."

   ❏ coach -"I am here to maximize the staff—not to play."

8. The *level of leadership* I would prefer to assume if I had my *preference* in an area of my confidence, on a team of equals, with time running out, and where a directional decision must be made would be (choose one)…

   ❏ president, executive director, head coach, senior pastor level

   ❏ assistant coach, associate pastor, vice-president level

   ❏ strong player, star player, etc., giving input to the direction but not making any final decisions

9. If I were given a *tough new assignment*, in the area of my competence I would actually *prefer*:

   ❏ starting with a *blank sheet of paper* and *originating* my own program that no one has ever seen before, including myself. ("If someone else has done it before why would I want to do it again?")

   ❏ being given two or three *successful models* which I could *adapt* into a new model that no one had seen and that was better than any of the rest. ("Why recreate the wheel?")

10. Candidly speaking, I would *feel most honored* to be thought of as:

    ❏ brilliant

    ❏ wise

    ❏ courageous

❏ faithful

❏ loyal

11. The three (nonbiblical) leaders in history (deceased or living) I *admire most* are:

_____

_____

_____

12. The *last three books* I bought with my own money were:

_____

_____

_____

13. The *last three audio* tapes I actually listened to were:

_____

_____

_____

I listened to them:

❏ in a group setting

❏ in my automobile

❏ in my study at home

❏ in my office

❏ other _____

Past Needs

14. If I could *start over* in my leadership development process, the first three things I *would try to master* would be:

_____

_____

_____

15. If I could *start over*, the three things I would *avoid at all costs* as a leader would be:

_____

_____

_____

Present Needs

16. My *ideal manager* would always:

_____

_____

_____

17. The greatest struggle I have in *managing other people* is:

_____

_____

18. The three things I would most like to *eliminate* from my current work responsibilities would be:

_____

_____

_____

19. The single thing I would most like to *change about myself*, if I could change anything, would be my:

_____

_____

20. The *three life concerns* that keep me awake at night or make me toss and turn are:

_____

_____

_____

21. If I could ask a *senior business adviser* just one question and knew I would get a sound answer about my *business*, I would ask:

_____

_____

22. If I could ask an *experienced wise psychologist,* just one question and knew I would get a profound answer about my *family or marriage,* I would ask:

_____

_____

23. If I could ask a *wise and trusted friend* just one question and knew I would get the answer about my *personal life,* I would ask:

_____

_____

24. If I could ask a *seasoned minister or theologian* just one question about *God,* I would ask:

_____

_____

25. As I define *what's holding me back* from reaching my full potential, I would say my *three greatest roadblocks* are:

_____

_____

26. I think my *confidence as a leader would double if* I could master:

_____

_____

_____

27. I would happily pay someone 10 percent *of my annual budget* to teach me how to:

_____

_____

_____

Future Needs

28. I would drive, fly, or walk a long way to *actually watch* and be able to ask questions of:

_____

29. The *single most important area* in which I would most like to *grow personally* in the future is:

_____

30. The *single greatest skill* I most need to learn to get *prepared for the future* is:

_____

31. Please rate the following topics as to your *felt need* for added help in these areas: (10=I feel a *great need* in this area, down to 1=I feel *little or no need* in this area.)

____ Accelerating the growth of our organization

____ Asking profound questions

____ Balance—maintaining personal balance

____ Birthday questions—questions to ask each year

____ Boardroom confidence

____ Brainstorming

___ Buddy—how to find and be one

___ Building a church building

___ Career change—questions to ask before making one

___ Cash flow projections—how to

___ Communicating effectively

___ Confidence—gaining/regaining

___ Coping with bad days

___ Consulting

    ___ How to find the right consultant

    ___ How to evaluate a consultant

    ___ How to become a consultant

___ Crisis—processing one

___ Decision making

___ Dreaming—how to define a life dream

___ Encouraging myself and others

___ Evaluating executives

___ Evaluating myself

___ Event planning

___ Filing effectively

___ Focusing life/priorities

___ Healthy organization checklist—audit

___ LifeWork

___ Marketing

___ Strategic Planning

___ Memories—capturing them for my family

___ Mentoring

_____ How to find a mentor

_____ How to become a mentor

_____ Niche—finding where I fit

_____ Partnerships

_____ How to form a partnership

_____ How to maximize a partnership

_____ How to get out of a partnership

_____ Pastoral search (executive search)

_____ Personal effectiveness

_____ Planning for the future

_____ Praying

_____ Pre-marriage counseling

_____ Presidential preparation

_____ Presidential profile—what to look for in a president

_____ Process charting—key to effectiveness and efficiency

_____ Public relations

_____ Relationships with:

_____ Children

_____ Father

_____ Mother

_____ Staff

_____ Social skills

_____ Social etiquette

_____ Speaking with confidence

_____ Staff meetings

_____ Starting a company

____ Starting a church

____ Stress

____ Succession

____ Tackling what seems to be impossible

____ Team leadership/Team building

____ Thinking for myself

____ Time management

____ Unconditional love

____ Why you do what you do

____ Writing my first book

32. I wish, sometime in the future, someone would *write books* on:

_____

_____

_____

33. I wish someone would do *videotapes* on:

_____

_____

_____

Free Forum

34. Free Forum: to *understand my needs fully* you really need to know that I...

_____

_____

_____

_____

Thank you for your candid responses!

Refinement – *Adaptable Samples*

G-1. Assimilation Process

Sample one:

MEMBERSHIP APPLICATION PROCESS

This process chart is attached to all membership applications. When each "position" is completed, the chart shall be noted and dated and passed along to the next person/stage of the membership process.

- ❏ Application received in office—chart attached
- ❏ Application given to office team
- ❏ Acknowledgment letter sent
- ❏ Application given to pastor's assistant for senior pastor file
- ❏ Pastor reads application and signs it
- ❏ Member class (attended) (excused)
- ❏ Application given to church board
- ❏ Interview with candidates(s) conducted
- ❏ Board approved and recommended
- ❏ Membership "checklist" given and reviewed
- ❏ Database survey

❏ Congregational vote

❏ Congratulations letter

❏ Gift book

❏ Welcomed at a morning service

❏ Name(s) added to membership rolls

❏ Host Family (linked for six-month follow-through)
After six months:

❏ Evaluated depth of assimilation

Sample two:

ASSESSING MY SPIRITUAL RESOURCES

I. Assessing My Resources

The work sheets on the following pages have been provided to help you in assessing who God made you to be and in identifying the unique resources He has entrusted to you. Work through each section honestly and as completely as possible. Relax and feel free to move on past any areas where you are unsure.

A. Spiritual gifts assessment

The New Testament does not give a procedure for personally discovering what your spiritual gifts are. It *assumes* that those gifts will practically emerge and become distinguishable as you grow in your relationship with God and as you actively serve Him. The only way to truly know your spiritual gifts is through repeated affirmation from the body of Christ. There are no tests, surveys, or assessments which can do that as effectively as the feedback from those in the church whom you serve. However, assessments can help indicate potential areas in which you are likely to have a spiritual gift.

The two best sources of input for determining your gifts are:

- what your *interests* and *desires* are as a growing, maturing, Spirit-filled Christian, and

- what others say that you do effectively.

When both of these sources of input strongly match, there is a good indication your gifts lie in that area. We want to encourage you to use two different types of assessments to help you begin to discover your gifts.

Directions: Read each of the descriptions below. Mark one of the following letters in the space provided.

D=Definitely true, yes, certain gift

P=Possibly true, maybe, potential gift

O=Not true, no observation

___ *Apostleship/Missionary:* The divine enablement from God to go into a new place and start and oversee the development of new churches

___ *Prophecy:* The divine enablement to proclaim God's truth with power and clarity in a timely and culturally sensitive fashion for correction, repentance, or edification

___ *Teaching:* The divine enablement to understand, clearly explain, and apply the truths of Scripture so others may learn and profit

___ *Exhortation/Encouragement:* The divine enablement to come alongside and strengthen, assure, affirm, or move in a godly direction those who are discouraged or who might be wavering in their faith

___ *Wisdom:* The divine enablement to make known the will of God as it applies to a specific situation

___ *Knowledge:* The divine enablement to make known information the Spirit wants revealed and which might otherwise be unknown

___ *Evangelism:* The divine enablement to effectively communicate the message of Christ to unbelievers in such a way that they respond in faith and discipleship

___ *Shepherding:* The divine enablement to lead, care for, and nurture individuals or groups in the body as they grow in their faith

____ *Discernment:* The divine enablement to distinguish between truth and error

____ *Giving:* The divine enablement to give an extraordinary portion of one's substance to the work of the Lord or to the people of God consistently, liberally, specifically, and with such wisdom and cheerfulness that others are encouraged and blessed

____ *Mercy:* The divine enablement to minister with cheerfulness and joy to the hurting, sick, anxious, poor, and sometimes undeserving within the body of Christ

____ *Faith:* The divine enablement to hold a vision of God's will and believe with unwavering confidence that God will work in spite of feelings or sometimes seemingly impossible circumstances

____ *Help/Service:* The divine enablement to serve faithfully behind the scenes in practical ways to assist in the work of the Lord and encourage and strengthen others spiritually

____ *Leadership/Administration:* The divine enablement to give direction and manage in such way that the work of ministry is accomplished effectively

B. Spiritual passion

A person's desires as a growing Christian often lead him to some compelling action. Your burden for unwed mothers, the poor, unbelievers, youth, discipleship, business executives, etc., is part of God's way of directing you to the place where you can best use your spiritual gifts. To identify and state your ministry motivation, carefully consider the following questions:

- Which local, global, political, social, or church issues cause a strong emotional stirring in you?

- To what groups of people do you feel most attracted?

- What needs around you would make you "weep and pound the table"?

- Assuming you have all the resources you need, and knowing you could not fail, what would you like to do in order to make a difference?

Conclude with a statement or use some key words to explain what you understand your ministry motivation to be at this time:

In light of the above, I would say I have the passion to...or for...

C. Abilities

- List any skills, talents, or special abilities below. Be honest and specific. After you have made a list, see if there are any items that can be grouped together in general categories.

- Describe two things you have done in the past (church, work, hobbies) that you enjoyed, gave you satisfaction, and you did well. Explain how you accomplished them.

D. Strengths

Out of the following words, circle the eight which would best describe you:

Determined	Independent	Optimistic	Practical
Decisive	Productive	Confident	Leader
Talkative	Outgoing	Enthusiastic	Friendly
Warm	Carefree	Compassionate	Personable
Calm	Dependable	Easygoing	Efficient
Conservative	Practical	Stable	Sympathetic
Gifted	Analytical	Sensitive	Perfectionistic
Aesthetic	Idealistic	Loyal	Self-sacrificing

E. Talents/Skills

God not only has given us spiritual gifts, but also has granted to each of us various talents, abilities, and skills. Both Christians and unbelievers have these. They can be developed through experience and education.

In what areas do you have a certain amount of competence? What do you do with confidence (i.e., athletics, catering, playing piano, carpentry, computer programming, gardening, etc.)?

II. Membership covenant

Believing that all people are sinful and that the just sentence of that sin is eternal separation from God (Romans 3:23; 6:23) and that Jesus Christ is God's only provision for man's sin (Romans 5:8) and having personally received Jesus Christ as my Savior and Lord (John 1:12, Revelation 3:20),

— and —

Having completed Discovery I and II, being committed to the doctrine, purpose, distinctives, and essentials of our church, I wish by the empowering of the Holy Spirit to enter into the following covenant with those who are part of this local church body:

1. I will seek to be conformed to the image of Christ through the four essentials for life change:

    - attending regular weekly *worship*,

    - involving myself in a *community* of spiritual relationships that brings mutual support and accountability to my life,

    - committing to *grow* in a lifestyle that manifests biblical truth, personal integrity (consistent with my spiritual beliefs), family as a priority, outreach to the community, and well-reasoned social involvement, and

    - taking the time to *serve* others in a manner that is consistent with my spiritual gifts.

2. I will support the ministry and witness of this local body to the community and the world by:

    - supporting others fervently in Christian love (1 Peter 4:8),

    - upholding others in prayer and bearing others' burdens during times of distress (Galatians 6:2), and

    - participating cheerfully and regularly in the financial support of the ministry and the obligations of the church (2 Corinthians 9:6–7).

3. I will seek to maintain the unity of the church body by:

- acting in love toward other members (1 Peter 1:22),

- seeking open and honest communication when I have concerns (Ephesians 4:15), and

- following the leadership of the church (Hebrews 13:17) and submitting to the principles of church restoration (Matthew 18:15–20).

Witnessed our hand and seal this _____ day of ____ , 20__.

Signature: _____ Witness:_____

Pastor: _____ Board Member _____

III. My Spiritual Journey

Where are you on your spiritual journey? In Colossians 2:6–7, Paul provides a good blueprint for considering this question. What different aspects of a person's growth can you identify in these two verses?

Sharing the Story of How I Received Christ

1. What was your life like before you received Christ?

2. How and when did you receive Christ as your Savior and Lord?

3. What has happened in your life since you trusted Christ?

Assessing My Progress on My Journey

A. Spiritual maturity

Each of us enjoys a different level of spiritual understanding. Growing in Christ takes time and requires our willingness to be conformed to His will. It is a process, a journey.

If you were to take a spiritual snapshot of your relationship with Christ, which of the following would best describe how you see yourself at this time? (Circle one. Be honest and fair in your evaluation.)

1. Searching/Seeking

   You are gaining a better understanding of Christ and the Christian faith, but you have not yet come to the place where you are personally trusting in Jesus for the forgiveness of your sins. You are still investigating Christianity. You are a seeker.

2. New/Young

   You have recently become a Christian. There is excitement and enthusiasm in your new walk with Jesus Christ, or you have been a Christian for a while, but you are just now becoming aware of what Jesus meant when He promised an abundant life. Whether a new or young believer, you still need to grow in your understanding of the basics of the Christian faith.

3. Growing/Stable

   You are confident in the faithfulness of God and His ability to accomplish His will in your life. You are teachable and sensitive to the Spirit's leading in your life. Your life is marked by the stability that comes from knowing Christ, regularly worshiping with His people, and being salt and light in the lives of others.

4. Leading/Guiding

   You have matured in the faith. You are able to model for other believers a life in Christ. You can lead by example and guide others in a deeper understanding of what it means to walk personally with God.

B. Spiritual training

(List your sources of spiritual training—Sunday school, church, small groups, seminary, personal study, etc.)

C. Spiritual knowledge assessment

(Assess your knowledge in each of the five areas from 1 to 5, 1 indicating little knowledge and 5 indicating much knowledge.)

___ *Assurance of salvation:* I can articulate with confidence the basis of my hope for salvation. This includes my confidence in the Bible as God's revelation to man, the basic nature of God, the work of

Christ, and how I came to know Him.

__ *Scope and significance of salvation:* I can explain the major aspects of salvation (depravity, regeneration, justification, sanctification, and glorification) and can articulate how those relate practically to life.

__ *Holy Spirit:* I have an accurate understanding of the Holy Spirit's identity and His presence both in the world and in the life of a believer. I am seeking to consistently walk in the Spirit.

__ *Spiritual warfare:* I understand the reality of spiritual conflict with Satan, demons, the world, and the flesh, and how to put on the full armor of God.

__ *Spiritual growth:* I understand the principles of spiritual growth and have developed a personalized plan for spiritual growth.

Based on your assessment, in which of the above areas of spiritual knowledge do you most need to grow?

D. Spiritual disciplines

(Assess your satisfaction with each of the following practices on a scale of 1 to 5, 1 being not very satisfied and 5 being very satisfied.)

__ *Lordship:* I am seeking to put Christ first in every area of life.

__ *God's Word:* I am practicing a consistent intake of God's Word through listening, reading, studying, memorizing, and meditating for the purpose of application to every area of my life.

__ *Prayer:* I have developed a lifestyle of consistent prayer.

__ *Witnessing:* I have become an effective witness for Jesus Christ by praying for and developing relationships with non-Christians, learning to share my personal testimony and a simple gospel presentation.

__ *Vision:* I have developed a servant's heart and am serving in an area of ministry which flows from my spiritual gifts and spiritual passion.

Based on your assessment, in which of the above spiritual disciplines do you most need to grow?

G-2. Facilities Cleaning Procedure

General Cleaning Procedure for Sunday Evenings

I. Downstairs

   A. Sanctuary

      1. Vacuum (weekly)

      2. General: straighten chairs, etc.

   B. Fellowship hall

      1. Vacuum (biweekly or after an event)

      2. Empty all trash into dumpster

      3. Wipe off all tables, kitchen counters—dispose of any food that has been left out

      4. General: straighten chairs, tables, etc.

   C. Rest rooms

      1. Clean inside of toilets with brush and toilet cleaner

      2. Clean outside of toilets with spray disinfectant

      3. Fill holders with toilet paper

      4. Fill toilet seat cover boxes

      5. Wipe stall doors, walls, ceramic tiling with spray disinfectant

      6. Empty sanitary boxes and trash, replacing with clean bags (empty all trash into dumpster)

      7. Clean mirror (if needed)

      8. Clean sinks with cleanser; countertops with spray cleaner

      9. Mop floors

      10. Leave doors open (to air out)

D. Foyer

    1. Vacuum (biweekly)

    2. General: straighten area

    3. Wash windows on front doors (when necessary)

E. Nursery and children's rooms

    1. Empty diaper pail(s)

    2. Dispose of any food that may have been left out

    3. Vacuum (biweekly)

    4. General: straighten area

II. Upstairs

A. Children and youth rooms

    1. Empty trash

    2. Dispose of any food that may have been left out

    3. Vacuum (biweekly)

    4. General: straighten area

B. Hallway

    1. Vacuum (biweekly)

G-3. Information Table Receptionist Procedure

Objective:

The objective of the Information Table and receptionist is to provide a friendly, effective means of welcoming our guests and members; answering questions (in person and on the telephone); familiarizing them with our church, ministries, and support which we provide; and a spot for event sign-ups and registrations.

I. Be friendly, approachable and personable with people

A. Smile, look approachable, remember that this is often the *first impression* of our church for our guests

    (1) Always keep the table neat and tidy looking

    (2) Answer telephone with "Good morning, [name of church], may I help you?"

II.   Knowledge of church events and leaders

    A. Have a general working knowledge of all events advertised on the Information Table

        1. Be prepared to answer questions or to direct people to the leader who can answer their questions

        2. Keep a current bulletin, a church calendar, and a ministries list with you at all times (attached)

III. Keep information current

    A. All general publications

        1. Keep supply on table for people to take

        2. Discard as dates expire or replace with new publications

    B. Brochures for conferences, seminars, etc.

        1. Keep supply on table for people to take. Discard as dates expire

        2. Do not accept any information for distribution unless it has been placed there by a church leader or personally approved by church administrator or another church leader

        3. Do not accept any information that does not directly apply to our church

        4. Keep a supply of our church business cards on the table

    C. Sign-ups and registrations for upcoming events

        1. Read bulletin on arrival; be sure that any sign-up sheets promised on the information table are actually there

2. If a sign-up or registration sheet is not there, contact either pastor, the ministry leader, or create a sheet for the event

IV. Working hours for receptionist

    A. Be at the information table at least *30 minutes before* and *15 to 20 minutes after* each service

        1. Table must be prepared *before* these times, so that when guests arrive you can be prepared to attend to them

        2. Prepare and train a backup person

            a. If you are not able to work at a particular time, you are responsible for providing a fully-trained back-up person

            b. Please notify the church administrator if possible (voice mail okay)

V. Other

    A. Please keep telephone hidden under desk at all times when Information Table is not occupied. Unplug cord from phone at phone base

    B. Please report all issues, problems, and ideas for improvement to the church administrator

G-4. Team Policy/Procedures Manual – Adaptable Sample

The following staff policy and procedure examples *may not be* fully valid or legal in your state. Employment laws vary from state to state. These samples are included here as a source of ideas, and examples of subjects that others have addressed.

Copy of (__Team Member's Name__)

Why a Team member Policy Manual?

Our church is pleased to present you with this team policy manual. It contains the basic statements about our approach to team relations. It describes our policy and summarizes benefits provided for you in addition to regular wages. If any questions arise regarding the interpretation of these policies, benefits, and/or plans, ask the church administrator.

This manual is yours to take home. It contains information of interest and importance to you and your family.

If you have any questions about any of the policies, procedures, or practices of our church, do not hesitate to ask your team leader for an explanation. If we have missed anything in preparing this manual, please let us have your questions.

The policies contained in this manual are not intended as a contract of employment and may be added to or changed as needed by our church at any time. Our church adheres to the policy of employment-at-will, which enables either the team member or the church to terminate the employment relationship at any time.

Confidential Information

Since we deal with personal information, each team member holds a position of trust. All records, reports, memoranda, and correspondence must be kept confidential (e.g., counseling information and/or files) and are the property of our church.

Unauthorized disclosure of any information or activities which may be detrimental to the interests of our church or members of the fellowship will be justification for dismissal.

SUBJECT: Equal Employment Opportunity

PURPOSE

To clearly state our church's objectives regarding equal employment opportunity

POLICY

Equal opportunity is our church's policy. It is our objective to select the best qualified person for each position in the organization.

No team member of our church will discriminate against a fellow team member or an applicant for employment on any legally recognized basis including, but not limited to, race, color, sex, national origin, non-position-related handicap, disability, age, or veteran status. This policy applies to all employment practices and personnel actions.

Conditions Of Employment

All team members and applicants of our church must be born-again believers and consider our church their home church.

Procedure

It shall be the responsibility of every team leader to promote the implementation of this policy and ensure conformance by their team.

Those responsible for hiring new team members must take all necessary actions in the elimination of discrimination toward team members and applicants for employment with our church in all categories and levels of employment and team member relations

Subject: Probationary Period

Purpose

The probationary period is an extension of the employment process and provides team leaders with the opportunity to evaluate team member performance and determine whether the individual is qualified for the position. Therefore, the performance of a team member will be subject to careful scrutiny and evaluation. Team members shall be informed of the probationary period before being hired.

Policy

Our church sets a 90-day probationary period for each new team member.

Procedure

The following procedures will govern team member benefits eligibility, performance appraisal, and termination during the probationary period.

1. Vacation and sick leave eligibility (if provided): Vacation and sick leave is calculated from the team member's date of hire. However, vacation may *not* be taken during the trial period, and then only after six months of service unless waived by the team leader or pastor.

2. Insurance Benefits (if provided): Insurance coverage is available for regular, full-time team members after a one-month service period.

3. Termination: Our church may release a team member at any time during the probationary period, without notice and without prejudice.

During the probationary period, a team member may terminate association with our church without notice and without prejudice.

At the end of the trial period a review is given to evaluate the progress and suitability of the individual for regular team member status. However, should a questionable situation arise during the probationary period, our church reserves the right to extend the probationary period for a reasonable length of time until such a determination can be made as to the reliability, capability, or suitability of the individual in question.

Subject: Employment Classification

Purpose

To state and define our church's employment classifications. Note: This is for classification purposes only, and not to define team member benefits.

Policy

All team members are classified as *exempt* or *nonexempt* according to the following definitions:

Salaried/Hourly Exempt—Positions of managerial, administrative, or professional nature as prescribed by federal and state labor statute which are exempt from overtime payments.

Salaried/Hourly Nonexempt—Positions of clerical, technical, or service nature, as defined by statute, which are covered by provisions for overtime payments.

There are then three subclassifications of team members. They are:

1. *Regular Full Time*—A team member who works at least 38 hours per week on a regularly scheduled basis.

2. *Regular Part Time*—A team member who works less than a 38-hour work week, on either a regularly scheduled basis or on an irregular basis.

3. *Temporary*—A team member hired for a period not exceeding three months and who is not entitled to regular benefits. An extension of temporary work classification for an additional three-month period or less may be granted, after review by management, if the assignment is found to be necessary. A temporary team member may be full-time or part-time. This classification applies to temporary maintenance, janitorial, secretarial, or clerical positions, as well as students working part-time and those who work during the summer.

Definitions:

Excused absence—Absence from work with the approval of the team leader. An excused absence may not exceed six (6) working days and must be for reasons such as the following: personal illness, illness or death in the immediate family, service as principal witness or juror, or annual military training. In any event a request for time off should be communicated and the purpose of the absence explained fully to the team leader not later than the first hour the team member is absent.

Layoff—Suspension of employment usually due to reduction of workload.

Leave of absence—Absence from work for a specific time and with reasonable assurance that work would be available at the end of the period. The time is more than seven (7) days and is granted for reasons such as: personal illness, pregnancy, formal education, military duty, etc. A leave of absence can be granted to permanent full-time team members only.

Unauthorized absence—Absence from work without the approval of the team leader.

SUBJECT: Working Hours

PURPOSE

To state and define our church's rules regarding working hours

POLICY

Because of the nature of our organization, your work schedule may vary depending on your position. Our normal business hours are as follows:

Office Hours: The regular office hours are from 9:00 a.m. until 5:00 p.m., Monday through Friday.

Lunch Periods: Team members have a paid lunch period of 30 minutes. Lunch periods should be arranged so adequate staff is present to provide the required services. Your team leader should be aware of your schedule.

Rest Breaks: You will be allowed one 15-minute rest break per half day worked. Breaks should be taken at mutually convenient times as worked out with your team leader.

The receptionist and your team leader should be informed of any appointments or time away from the office. It is very important that the receptionist has knowledge of your schedule and location to ensure a proper response to people on the phone.

SUBJECT: Overtime and Compensatory Time

PURPOSE

To state and define our church's rules regarding overtime and compensatory time

POLICY

No overtime permitted; compensatory time is preferred.

Overtime: As defined by the Federal Fair Labor Standards Act, professional team members and team members in team leader and management positions are "exempt" team members. If you are an exempt team member, you are not paid for overtime worked. Non-exempt team members who work overtime are paid time-and-a-half for more than eight hours in a work day and double time for more than twelve hours in a work day. In a work week more than 40 hours is paid time-and-a-half.

Compensatory time: If you are a non-exempt team member all overtime hours should be cleared with your immediate team leader prior to their occurrence and compensatory time scheduled with your team leader to be taken as soon as the schedule permits.

SUBJECT: Reporting Absences

PURPOSE

To state and define our church's rules regarding absences and time away from work

POLICY

If you are ill and not able to work, you should call your office manager by 9:00 a.m. Should the phone not be answered due to staff prayer, you should call immediately after 9:30 a.m. All absences must be for good and sufficient reason. The fact that you have notified your team leader that you will be gone does not necessarily make it an approved or paid absence.

When you know ahead of time that you will be absent, you should make the necessary arrangements in advance with your team leader.

If you plan to return to work on a definite date but are unable to do so, it is your responsibility to notify your team leader to this effect.

If you are absent from work for three (3) consecutive work days without notifying your team leader, it will be considered that you have voluntarily terminated employment.

SUBJECT: Holidays

PURPOSE

To provide team members with paid time away from their positions for recreation, rest, and relaxation

POLICY

Our church observes and pays for holidays as follows:

1. New Year's Day
2. Memorial Day
3. Fourth of July
4. Labor Day
5. Thanksgiving Day
6. Friday after Thanksgiving Day
7. Christmas

When a holiday falls on a Saturday, it will be observed on the preceding Friday. Holidays that fall on a Sunday will be observed on the Monday following.

Team members must work the last scheduled day before the holiday and the first scheduled working day following the holiday in order to be eligible for holiday pay unless time off on these days has been excused. Only regular, full-time team members are eligible for full holiday pay.

If a holiday falls within a team member's vacation period, the holiday is not considered a vacation day.

SUBJECT: Work Performance and Conduct

PURPOSE

To establish and define a uniform policy pertaining to marginal and substandard performance or conduct

POLICY

While it is preferable to keep rules and regulations to a minimum, there are some which are necessary for the efficient operation of our church. It is impossible to provide an exhaustive list that identifies every type of conduct or performance problem that may result in disciplinary action. However, in order to offer team members some guidance, the following examples illustrate types of conduct that are *not* in the best interest of either our church or its team members and which, therefore, are not permitted and may result in disciplinary action up to and including discharge:

1. Habitual tardiness or absenteeism

2. Falsifying or altering church records

3. Theft or misuse of church or personal property

4. Disorderly conduct on church premises, such as, but not limited to, fighting, using foul language, possessing alcohol or narcotics

5. Distribution of literature or solicitation on church premises for unapproved causes

6. Unauthorized personal use of church equipment or property

7. Inefficient or careless performance of duties: failure to maintain standards of workmanship

8. Unauthorized departure from responsibilities or church premises

9. Insubordination (refusal to do work assigned *or* repeated requests to comply ignored)

10. Involvement in the initiation, authorship, or transmittal of

a threatening or defamatory communication, either written or oral, concerning the church or its team members

11.   Loitering or sleeping on the position

12.   Sexual harassment or sexual misconduct

13.   Illegal or criminal activity, such as illegal drug use or abuse of prescription drugs, rape, murder, kidnapping, etc.

14.   Unauthorized disclosure of any information or activities which may be detrimental to the interests of our church or members of the fellowship

SUBJECT: Terminations

PURPOSE

To aid management in handling the responsibilities associated with the removal of an team member from the payroll and to ensure uniform separation practices and fairness to both parties

DEFINITIONS

A. *Resignation*—Resignation is always voluntary and includes:

- resignation with or without notice

- an absence of three or more consecutive working days without notice to your team leader at the church

B. *Release*—Not adapted for the type of work and no other assignments available, or lack of qualifications required. Release usually results from no fault of the team member; rather it signifies a mismatch of position requirements and team member skills. Team members who are unable to perform satisfactorily during the probationary period will also be considered released.

C. *Retirement*—Self-explanatory

D. *Layoff*—Layoff includes:

- temporary layoff. No work available and recall expected within twelve months

- permanent layoff. No work available and recall not expected

E. *Discharge*—Team member who is removed from payroll for violation of team member standards of conduct, safety regulations, or unsatisfactory position performance for which the team member is at fault.

PROCEDURE

A. *Layoff*—If termination is due to layoff, up to two weeks' notice *may* be given to team member. Team members scheduled for layoff will be expected to continue their work during this period.

B. *Release*—If a team member is to be released, up to one week's notice *may* be given at the option of the church.

C. *Resignation*—A team member who resigns should complete a letter of resignation. This notice will be given to the team leader who will forward it to the proper person for filing in the team member's personnel folder. Our church requests two (2) weeks' notice of resignation.

D. *Discharge*—When a team member is to be discharged, the team leader must have the approval of the senior pastor.

E. *Benefits Eligibility*—When a team member is separated for any reason, except for layoff, team member benefit credits are lost with these exceptions:

- Vacation—Accrued but unused vacation allowance will be paid to team members, provided they have completed the probationary period.

- Health benefits (if provided)—Group insurance coverage will cease at the time of termination. However, the team member has the option to convert to individual life or health coverage at the team member's expense.

F. *Exit interview*—Every team member who terminates from our church will attend an exit interview. At this time the team member will return all items belonging to our church (keys, manual, credit cards, etc.) and receive the final paycheck after all outstanding debt or obligations are deducted.

SUBJECT: Personal Problems/Complaints

"Open Door Policy"

PURPOSE

To ensure every team member is treated justly and equitably at all times

POLICY

Our church has always given utmost consideration to the well-being of its team members. If a team member has a personal problem concerning a work-related matter, our church welcomes and encourages the team member to follow the procedure below.

PROCEDURE

1. First the problem should be discussed with the team member's immediate team leader. An important part of a team leader's responsibility is to see that the team member is treated fairly and equitably at all times through consistent administration of our church's policies.

2. If, after discussion of the problem with the team leader, the team member is not satisfied with their assistance offered, an "open door" policy exists which gives the team member complete freedom to take the problem to the senior pastor.

3. If the problem is of a *pastoral* nature, such as spiritual, non-work related, etc., then you are encouraged to seek pastoral care from your home fellowship leader or appropriate staff pastor.

SUBJECT: Performance Review and Salary Merit Increase

PURPOSE

To ensure a review process that is workable, equitable, and as objective as possible

POLICY

All team members of our church will participate in a performance review with the team leader based on the following schedule:

1. On completion of probationary period and every July thereafter.

2. As often as is warranted by the positional situation and the team member's performance.

The performance review will be completed in writing after the completion of the interview between the team member and her/his team leader. The team member is encouraged to share in the review process by adding written comments to the evaluation.

The team leader will determine when and if a merit increase is warranted. It is our church's policy to reward team members with a periodic merit increase in salary for dedication in their work, extra effort, and better-than-average performance. Management does not award merit increases on an automatic basis or at any preset interval.

The team member is encouraged to:

1. Inquire about her/his performance.

2. Accept additional responsibilities and show initiative.

3. Learn about training available to assist the team member in skills improvement.

SUBJECT: Team member Benefits

PURPOSE

Team member benefits play a vital role in providing income security. They form an important part of your compensation. Our church annually looks for ways to make desirable and justifiable changes in our benefit plans.

Policy

After enrollment, any team member working a minimum of 38 hours per week will complete the form requesting team member benefits.

If a team member does not wish to participate in our church's group insurance plan, the waiver portion of the enrollment cards must be completed.

Summary Of Benefits:

Group Insurance Benefits (life, medical, dental)

Eligibility and effective date: Eligible team members for the group life, medical, and dental benefits are as follows:

1. Permanent full-time team members who qualify as head of household for income tax purposes are eligible to receive team member and dependent coverage.

2. Permanent full-time team members who do not qualify as head of household for income tax purposes are eligible for team member coverage, unless approved by the Finance Committee or Senior Pastor.

3. Eligible team members are qualified for the life, medical, and dental insurance benefits on the first day of the month following a full month of employment (see the following examples):

Date of hire	*Effective date*
January 1	February 1
January 16	March 1
January 31	March 1

Life Insurance Benefits

1. Coverage for eligible team members (as stated above) is available in the amount of $25,000.

Medical Insurance Benefits

1. Eligible team members (as stated earlier) are offered medical insurance.

2. Please refer to the available booklet, which describes the benefits and limitations in detail.

Dental Insurance Benefits

1. Dental insurance is available to eligible team members (as stated earlier) and dental care is provided by our assigned dentist *only*.

2. The dental benefit plan begins January 1 and runs through Dec.31.

3. See the available detailed description of benefits for more information.

Workers' Compensation Insurance

1. Workers' compensation insurance pays all medical, surgical, and hospital expenses in addition to a weekly benefit with the fourth day of disability caused by work-related injury or illness. Payment is made from the first day of the hospitalization if you are hospitalized before the fourth day or unable to work for more than 14 days.

2. You must report any work-related injuries or illnesses to your team leader immediately.

3. This plan is integrated with our church's sick leave plan to provide full pay as long as sick leave accrual lasts. Our church pays the entire cost of workers' compensation insurance beginning on the first day of employment.

Social Security

All team members, except pastors, are required by law to participate in Social Security under the Federal Insurance Contributions Acts (FICA), which provides for a fixed monthly retirement benefit, disability benefits if totally and permanently disabled, and certain survivors' benefits to dependents when a team member dies. The cost of this program is established by law and changes from time to time. Our church contributes a tax equal to the team member's contributions, except for pastors who are self-employed and pay all of their applicable FICA (SECA) tax.

Unemployment and State Disability Insurance

Team members do not accrue benefits under unemployment or state disability insurance due to our church's nonprofit status. Therefore, there is no unemployment compensation for one who leaves the employ of our church after the 90-day probationary period. Unemployment compensation, if any, for a team member who leaves within the 90-day probationary period would be determined by the team member's previous employer.

SUBJECT: Sick/Personal Leave

PURPOSE

To provide income protection for team members during temporary periods of illness or injury

POLICY

Our church provides six (6) sick/personal leave days per year to all *full-time* team members. Part-time team members will earn sick or personal leave at half the full-time rate. Temporary team members are not eligible for sick/personal leave.

PROCEDURE

1. A team member may take sick/personal leave after satisfactory completion of the probationary period.

2. Sick/personal leave is granted from date of hire at the rate of four (4) hours per month (pro-rated for part-time).

3. Sick leave is accrued on the last day of the month. Team members must be on active pay status on the last day of the month in order to accrue sick leave for that month.

4. A team member on a leave of absence does not earn sick leave.

5. Maximum sick/personal leave grant is six days and is *not* accrued from year to year. If not used, it will not be paid.

6. Time for routine doctor or dentist appointments is not to be charged to sick leave. Team members should make such appointments before or after work for that day if possible. Arrangements for time off for such appointments, if necessary, should be made with the team member's team leader in advance.

7. *A team member must personally call* her/his team leader to inform the team leader of illness if the team member cannot make the regularly scheduled work day.

SUBJECT: Vacation

PURPOSE

To provide team members paid time away from their positions to afford them the opportunity for rest, relaxation, and recreation

POLICY

Permanent, full-time team members who have satisfactorily completed the 90-day probationary period are eligible for paid vacation time as follows:

1. Non-exempt team members are eligible for:

   a. one week accrued during the first year

   b. two weeks after one year of continuous service

   c. three weeks after five years of continuous service

2. Exempt team members are eligible for:

   The same vacation time as established above unless other arrangements are made in writing prior to the beginning of the vacation accrual year. Regular part-time team members are not eligible for paid vacation time.

ALL TEAM MEMBERS

Team members may take vacation at any time throughout the year. All vacations must be scheduled and approved in advance with the team leader.

A team member's vacation time vests when it is accrued and cannot be carried over to future calendar years if not taken.

QuickWisdom.com

AN INTRODUCTION...AND AN INVITATION!

As an executive mentor/consultant, I have the rare privilege of spending days at a time with some of the finest leaders of our generation. I continue to grow personally, learning more in the past year than I've learned in the five years before it.

Mentoring Realities

In my book *Mentoring*, I define mentoring ideally as "a life-long relationship in which the mentor helps the protege grow into her/his God-given potential over a lifetime." Realistically, because of schedule pressures, my personal mentoring is limited to a very few individuals. At the same time, I truly want to see friends like you grow into your God-given potential over your lifetime.

Solomon advised, "Get Wisdom."

The search of today seems to be focused on becoming a courageous, charming, powerful, successful person. However, according to the Bible, Solomon, who was one of the wisest, if not the wisest, man that ever lived, gave us this profound and timeless bit of advice in Proverbs 4:5...GET WISDOM!

This is advice that our modern world seems to overlook.
Enter the idea of **Quick Wisdom.**

The focus of **Quick Wisdom** is to help you and your friends be WISE!

Today, it seems to me that every young leader I meet wants wisdom, but needs it fast. We don't have the time with today's pace and pressures to go to a mountaintop and study ancient manuscripts in Sanskrit. Thus—"Quick Access to Timeless Wisdom." My focus: 3-10 times per month I plan to send "QuickWisdom" emails to pass on the very best "wisdom nuggets" I can give you each month to help strengthen you and your friends.

Free to you and your friends.

Quick Wisdom is 100% free to you and your friends.

Fortunately, the email technology of today is such that you can enroll 10 friends or 100 to receive the **Quick Wisdom** email. It takes me the same amount of time to send you an email as it does to send it to all of your proteges/friends. I want to use my unique exposure to great wisdom to strengthen you and your friends for a lifetime.

Thank you, my friend, for telling your friends about **Quick Wisdom. com**!

www.QuickWisdom.com